One4DeBrovahs

Author: cheo jeffery allen solder
www.cheosolder.com
Trilingual Press / PO Box 391206 / Cambridge, MA 02139

Tel. 617-331-2269
Email: trilingualpress@tanbou.com

Cover Photo & Graphic design: Anna Grichting Solder

Production support: David Henry

ISBN 13: 978-1-936431-04-5
ISBN 10: 1-9364310-4-1

Library of Congress Control Number: 2012938019
Printed in the United States
First edition:
October 2013

One4DeBrovahs

cheo jeffery allen solder

Trilingual Press, Cambridge, Massachusetts

TABLE OF CONTENTS

Acknowledgements	7
Reviews	9
Introduction	11
I. MIND	13
1. katrina, katrina, oh rita	15
2. boston, outside in	29
3. sedition	41
4. sticks and stones	55
5. race, race, racing	65
6. are they mad?	73
7. london bridge is falling down	81
II. HEART	91
8. honey baby	93
9. the king is dead but not forgotten	99
10. snapshots	115
III. SPIRIT	127
11. two emperors	129
12. saint alice	133
13. my god, by god	139

ACKNOWLEDGEMENTS

acknowledgments (...first read but last written...)

to even begin to thank the many, many people who have contributed to the writing of this work is a mind boggling task...

to writers who have come before me and left footprints far too big for me to fill but whose very giant imprint on my mind, heart and spirit gave me a trail to dog, i say a heartfelt but simple and humbled thank you.

to family, both home and world flung, it is you i represent here as best i can and again, thank you ever so much.

to abu who took the time to risk a friendship with his quiet, intelligent, wise and totally unappreciated two cents... ...well, i lied. i think you know i did...

to my fellow artists at trilingual press, who have gathered me into the fold at last... thank you ever so much for your kindness, attention and confidence.

to love, in the person of anna who has never wavered in her support of crazy me, i cannot even begin to form the words sufficient to my gratitude.

REVIEWS

What one gets from reading One4DeBrovahs

"I am like a mild volcano waiting to erupt," [said one man]. This is what one gets from reading One4DeBrovahs ... I felt from reading the early chapters that I was waiting for the volcano to erupt based on his analysis of racial and class issues in the United States. He angrily confronts us with the stark reality of our government's destructive activities both here and abroad.

...He is particularly appreciative of the strength of the women and their role in his maturing. The stage is then set for his travels which have him meet the "Emperor of Ethiopia," "The Lion of Judah," and his sharing of his musical talents on a mystical spiritual journey with Alice Coltrane. "

Mel King, Professor MIT, Politician and Community Activist, Founder of the South End Technology Center, Boston.

"Solder creates a mosaic, a crimson rhapsody..."

" Cheo Solder's writing issues from the fluidity of his consciousness. He offers the gift of an unwavering eye seeking compassionate justice, and he does it with the wisdom of life lived deeply with all its dangers. These are words that will allow apologies before they grant forgiveness. Scanning the history of black people with a rootedness in his personal challenges, Solder creates a mosaic, a crimson rhapsody that is more jazz than blues, but as inclusive as one can imagine when weighing the necessity of the gospel of jazz and of the spirituality of the blues. He writes to an energetic theater that would awaken us while awakening the theater itself, where the seeds of the growth of a people live."

Afaa Michael Weaver, Simmons College, Boston.

INTRODUCTION

after many years absent from the scene of the creative arts, one morning not long ago, i woke up on a warm boston saturday and decided that i needed to get back to myself and needed to get to work on what i was born to do. i left my apartment and went in search of a music store. after a bit i found one that sold the type of instruments that i used to play and i found out how much it would cost me to buy an alto flute. i waited until i had a few extra dollars and returned to the store to put money down, though i did not have the full amount. a few months later i was the owner of a beautiful instrument and for the first time in over fifteen years, i began to play again.

i also started to write again. i had not written a serious poetic word in the same length of time. the funny thing is that this time, instead of poetry, prose poured out onto the page. it felt the same to write it as it did when i wrote poetry. the same tears fell on the pages and the same swelling of my heart took place so i kept at it. eventually, an idea began to form in my head of a collection of words and music to be performed on a stage as a set piece. a set of pieces talking about manhood and things related: how to get there, how to stay there and perhaps, just perhaps how to grow beyond manhood to humanhood.

i write out of the need to get it out, these thoughts that rocket round my skull and i write because i think that what i know may be of some small use to a generation that has largely ceased to talk about important things. you may agree or not agree with me in ways both big and small but the very action of thinking about it long enough to come to a conclusion about it is the beginning of the process of finding solutions to our collective problems. we need to talk to each other and we need to talk about things more serious than the latest fashion, fad, song or championship ring.

one4debrovahs is a collection of thoughts written during the later part of 2005 and the early part of 2006. it is offered with humility and love to you, my brothers and sisters and i hope that it has some use. that is my most sincere and greatest wish, that it has some use.

blessings of peace,

cheo jeffery allen solder

PART I. MIND

One4DeBrovahs

MIND

katrina, katrina, oh rita

sounds like a couple of good time girls, doesn't it? while the names are quite as american as apple pie or tom, dick and harry or sally may or jane, they also have the flavor spanish. i have known a few ritas' and one or two katrinas' in my time. maybe rita is the name of a friendly waitress who calls you "hon" while serving up your flapjacks or maybe she's an old time switchboard operator in the black and white films of the thirties or forties. katrina has flashing white teeth in her smile, slashing colorful full skirts and twirls while she dances, maybe she wears a flower in her long, thick hair. recent times notwithstanding, i think my opinion hasn't changed that much. they are still nice names, conjure warm and familiar images. don't judge a book by its cover, the old folks say.

when i saw this latest and most murderous katrina's waters covering new orleans on cnn that first day, i think i was more amazed than anything else. i knew that the city was below sea level. i have family and friends from there and i replayed a conversation that i once had with a creole girlfriend. she told me that everyone was buried above ground in vaults in n'awlins, not in the cold, cold dirt like in los angeles, my home town, and that the graveyards there only allowed the dead to rest in place for a year and one day. after the year and the day the remains are removed and stored in a box, in order to make way for the more recently dead as space is limited. this is because the old and crowded french city is below sea level and that digging graves in the ground was problematic. if you tried it, you were very likely to come up with a hole full of seawater. it was just a passing moment in a passing conversation but i remember it because it was strange and new to me.

but, that day i guess i was glued to my seat like everyone else in range of a television. as the hours passed, i saw many soul wrenching sights and i shed more than a few tears of sympathy and empathy. people waving flags and rags from rooftops, wading through muddy waters to dubious safety at the now not-so-super super dome and so many, far too many, finally just floating face down; all of it was more than enough to break the hardest among us down to wanting to jump on the nearest fast moving transport and rush to the rescue with long ropes, hot food, dry clothes and canteens. bless you sean penn, john travolta and those others who did just that.

now, i've grown up in america and seen other disasters unfold, for sure. i've been in earthquakes in southern california too numerous to mention. i have seen a terrible tornado at a close but safe distance. i've lived through a hurricane. i have gone through snowstorms and blizzards aplenty. i have even waded through high waters myself when a dam broke near my home when i was in high school.

i watched the space shuttle blow up that time because i had just bought a new television set and the technician, who was setting it up, had turned it on to see if everything was a-ok and it just happened to be on the right channel and about ten seconds later the shuttle made a beautiful white cloud and smoke design in the blue sky right before our startled eyes.

i had an office on the 53rd floor of the empire state building up until about four months before 9/11 and would have certainly had a ringside seat for that because i always got to the office early and my curtainless office windows faced the world trade center. as it happened, i watched it on cnn international while in germany. i saw the second plane hit live and in living color and i saw the buildings fall down a few minutes later.

from the long and safe distance of television, i have seen the dazed and bewildered trying to explain what they have gone through. from 9/11, for instance, i still remember this hospitalized young sister's breathless shell shocked stream of consciousness telling of how she was fleeing down the stairs of the world trade center and how she was trapped in the stairwell as it suddenly collapsed around and on top of her and the prayers and thoughts that were going through her mind at the time and how she was preparing to die in as much peace as possible and had just prayerfully given herself over to god's safe keeping hands and then, how in the dark, she heard a faint tapping sound through the impossible wall of plaster, concrete and twisted steel and thought to herself maybe i am not dead yet and desperately tapped an answer back and how some blessed souls then slowly reached her and carefully dug her out and brought her to the hospital. with her face mostly a mosaic of scars and bandages, she told of all this like it was happening all over again; her voice was smoke damaged, injured; a harsh yet light and young whisper with which she talked faster and faster and told the whole story in one breath, it seemed, and then exhausted from the effort of recounting her forever memories, she lay her head back on the soft pillow of her healing place and just stared at the unflinching camera and beyond.

i know i had stopped breathing, just listening to her story and i was re-living it with her. i too tasted the terror of the downward flight away from the flames and through the choking smoke, i too heard the sudden terrible noises of the stairwell giving way, i too felt the weight of the stones on my own broken legs and damaged body, i too understood the reaching out to heaven, knowing these were my last moments and then i too knew the incredible rush of joy and gratitude that she must have known when they reached into the rubble and touched her outstretched fingers before they got to the rest of her and i too cherished, just like her, the wonderful fact that some kind one held and patted her hand and didn't let go until they had her out, safe and away. tears coursed down her one cheek that was visible through the bandages and down both of my unharmed and unscarred cheeks and i thanked brave men and women and god for her life and then i cried for all the lost ones leaping or burned, for all the brave firemen and selfless policemen who were more than just doing their jobs when they perished, trying to help others to safety as the buildings collapsed.

and - i remember watching the news of the big san francisco earthquake a few years back and i remember seeing that a freeway overpass had fallen down and had flattened many cars that happened to be passing under it at the time. the people in the cars were mostly dead, crushed by the weight of that entire quake broken and shattered concrete but some were still alive and were weakly calling out for help. these people were doomed. there were fires spreading under there. you could hear the explosions as the gas tanks went, one by one. i remember getting on my knees and praying to god to forget about me and the rest of us for a little while, we were fine but if he could pay some extra special attention to those poor souls trapped in that hell in the city by the bay, it would be a good thing to do and a good time to do it. i have a very vivid imagination. i must have cried and prayed for an hour. i still pray for them every now and again.

i don't usually watch tv. i have more than enough nonsense in my head without filling it up with stuff that either makes not a jot of difference to me or - worse - stuff that i cannot do anything about even if it does make a difference to me. i think this is the result of watching fascism openly take hold in the land of my birth. i won't call it my country because i don't believe that it is my country. i believe that i am just like the native "americans" who are still today being kept on reservations; i believe that i am, like my red brothers and sisters, a prisoner of war. they may live here but that don't make them no americans. and us - africans who were finally freed from four hundred years of slavery are no americans either, even if we don't know it. as far as i am concerned, generally speaking, this has always been true but the last few years, things have really gone south. no pun intended, sorry.

i am accustomed to being ignored. they ain't got nothin' for us. these folks who are truly americans would be very happy if we all went back to africa or just went some-goddamned-where, anyway. this is true in the best of times. we are used to it, though. we may not like it much but we are used to it. life is never easy on us. the breaks don't come our way often. even during fat times, we usually stare at slim days, wishing for just a little bit more, not as much as everybody else seems to be getting, no, that would be too much to ask and we know it, but just enough extra so we can breathe a little easier, is all we are really asking.

sure, there are the bill cosbys and berry gordys and oprahs among us. some of us are blessed to be fast or funny or really smart or strong or lucky or something out of the ordinary and sometimes we get over a little. believe me when i say a little. a billion bucks is a lot of green to you and me, maybe, but it is still small potatoes in the real world. and - it does not bring power with it.

in general, though, our people are not rich. we are poor and struggling. we are passed over for promotions. we cannot get the cushy jobs if we can get a job at all. our reality is very different. all you have to do is to drive though the nearest ghetto and then drive through the nearest white area and the difference is as plain as the nose on your face. our schools are substandard. our businesses are small. our homes are small and raggedy. trash litters our streets. drugs and alcohol litter our minds. early graves rush most of us. either we kill ourselves with foolishness or we die of stress related illnesses. a person can take only so much after all, after all, a person can take only so much.

this is the normal state of things and it has been thus since slavery ended. but - what i saw on tv that day, my people begging for salvation, drowning and dying right before my tear filled gaze was way beyond the normal state of things.

i remember the note someone pinned to the corpse of a lost woman left on the street under a tarp, a note telling her name and adding "god help us" because they could not do anything more for her. i remember the mayor screaming in frustration for help, saying what needed to be said. i remember a woman reporter on cnn dismissing somebody else on air with her at the time who said something represented "good news". i don't remember the statement that prompted it but, in response, she incredulously asked: "how can you describe anything that we are seeing as good news? when people are dying right before our eyes? when people are drowning or being eaten by alligators, what can possibly be good news about that?" i remember the shock of thinking about alligators in louisiana and the poor folks in the water with them. they are one of my personal most frightening creatures (the damned things can run thirty five – forty miles an hour, climb trees and even jump rather high and they have all those teeth to boot) and there are a lot of them in louisiana and a flood rings the dinner bell, y'all. there are still thousands of people missing. thousands. they don't talk about that one much.

and then, i remember the picture of bush happily strumming his new guitar in california while the worst of this was going on and then, finally, after a few missteps and missed chances, i remember the story and the pictures of his fly by some days later in air force one, looking out of the tiny window at the devastation below and commenting that from up here, it looked like quite a mess down there. from up here. i remember his moment with brownie. i remember him and his rolled up sleeves, striding along, trying to look concerned and in charge and the brother mayor looking like he was trying to restrain himself from kicking the president's sorry ass. i remember him passing out ice. maybe that was another time. it might have been rita's turn for center stage. i might be confusing photo ops but i remember thinking, whenever it was, whichever disaster it was (and weren't there quite a few on his watch? what was up with that? was god trying to tell us something?), i remember thinking: "why is the president passing out ice, ain't he got more important stuff to do?" this time, though, for sure it was katrina, i remember him hugging two weeping haile berry looking sisters. shit, i admit it. i would have hugged them too. they were fine and i am still a man. i had to smile and give him that one. i couldn't help it. it was the first thing i'd found to smile about in days. a person can only take so much.

beyond that...

it was a wake up call. no, it was a wake the fuck up call. no, it was a wake the fuck up, slap you upside your head and a stomp on your sore foot wake up scream, not just a call, a wake the fuck up scream. if you watched all that unfold, like i did and it did not jolt you out of whatever stupor most of us are in, then something is seriously wrong with you. check your pulse, 'cause you are probably dead and are just too dumb to get it yet. go lie down. rest in peace. that's what dead people do. body dead, brain dead; what's the damned difference?

those of us who are still on our feet, however, have a problem. how do we react? what should we do? we now know that the reference to the straggling survivors as refugees was no unfortunate slip of the tongue, even if they did try to clean it up a few days later. they were refugees and so are we all.

that much was made crystal clear. we are the survivors of the greatest crime history has ever known. hundreds of millions of us perished under the back breaking work, the killing sun and slaver's whips and we are the descendents of the survivors. we were freed from bondage but never restored to freedom. we have been barely subsisting in a purgatory like state ever since, neither heaven nor hell, exactly. betwixt and between, if you will…

katrina showed just how little distance we have traveled in all this time, after all this effort. we can thank her for that at least; for showing us the truth and for allowing us to drop the scales and blinders from our eyes. that she also revealed that the country was bankrupt was another benefit. in all fairness to brownie, the cupboards were bare. since when did we need doctors, food, medical supplies and even water from other countries?

the country was raped and bled dry by that current pack of thieves. between iraq and afghanistan and all the sweetheart deals, the united states of america is in hock up to its eyeballs, mostly to china. if this was a business, we would be in receivership, trying to explain what went wrong and to work it out with a judge's help. so be it. that, however, is not my issue. america and i have very different issues. my issues have to do with my response on a very personal and selfish level. it is time for us to realize that we alone are responsible for us and our continued survival. if america survives, we are still in grave danger and always have been and always will be.

but…

what to do? what to do? i may not know all the answers to that one but i do know a few things that we need to ponder right away.

"when in the course of human events, it becomes necessary for one people to dissolve the political bands which have connected them with another, and to assume among the powers of the earth, the separate and equal station to which the laws of nature and of nature's god entitle them, a decent respect to the opinions of mankind requires that they should declare the causes which impel them to the separation."

first off, our newest and next phase of the "movement" should begin with a tax revolt.

if any of us ever pay another dime in taxes, then we are fools who deserve whatever happens to fools who refuse to face the truth staring them right in the face, fools who continue to believe in fantasy. i say, simply refuse to pay any more money into a system that is rigged against us. taxation without representation was the cry in the 1700's. it should be our cry now. dare them to lock us all up. all thirty – forty million of us - lock us up, if they can. we should not go quietly either. make it a war, if we have to. they ain't the only ones with guns. gladiator school has taught our young men and women to fear nothing and no one. and hard and long life has taught those of us who are older that there is nothing to fear anyway. death comes to us all in the end. and – don't forget - half of the army is us.

"we hold these truths to be self-evident, that all men are created equal, that they are endowed by their creator with certain unalienable right; that among these are life, liberty and the pursuit of happiness."

we should also be thinking about getting out of here. not to europe and not to south america where we also aren't wanted. we should be thinking about going home at long last. africa is waiting and needs us and our energy and knowledge. i don't know if anybody is taking note, but the home front is not doing too hot these days. aids, civil wars, genocide, rape, corruption, drought and starvation are all plaguing our homeland and it is not necessary. africa could very well be the richest continent on the face of the earth and it could easily be the richest and most powerful nation on the face of the earth if unified. read diop's "black africa" if you don't believe me. garvey, dubois, malcolm and many others have had the same thought so it is not new, it is just time.

"but when a long train of abuses and usurpations, pursuing invariably the same object evinces a design to reduce them under absolute despotism, it is their right, it is their duty, to throw off such government, and to provide new guards for their future security."

i know. you are rolling your eyes. africa. what do we know about africa? i can hear you thinking. i remember the fights when i was a little kid growing up in watts and somebody called somebody else a black african. i know that the natives in the tarzan movies shamed us with their bones through their noses. i know that the cartoon caricatures with their puffy, pink lips and black skin and funny shaped long heads always looked so ugly and all that. please realize that we have been trained by mis-education and carefully thought out propaganda to be ashamed of our african origins and the images are not real. africans are just as beautiful and/or just as ugly as anybody else anywhere. look around you. and africa itself is beautiful beyond words or compare. the vast grasses, the deep valleys, the running rivers and rich earth call to us to come home, can't you hear it? leaving in the first place was not our idea, remember? we mourned the loss of her, locked away in the belly of those terrible ships long ago, remember?

a modern africa does not have to be the deep, dark jungle of your worst fears. it can include big cities that look just like paris, hong kong or new york, only our version can be with pyramids and skyscrapers side by side and without the ghettoes. we could build a new n'awlins full of light laughter and music, since it is the people who shed the light and make the music, not the geographic locale.

a modern africa can include farmlands that grow many things, not just cassava and roots, whatever they are. it can include super highways where you can tool in your rides that can be manufactured there too. chrysler's award winning best car was designed by a brother. the natural resources are all there. we have invented many of the modern conveniences, like the elevator. why should we stop now? read your history.

i also know that you ain't ready to go anywhere; that you really think that this is your country too and you ain't going to nobody's africa, in any case. it's too hot. i can hear you thinking.

ok. then stay and die, fools. think back to germany and to how many wise jews read the handwriting on the walls and got out of dodge before things got too far out of hand. what happened to those who did not go? think about england and how and why the pilgrims came here in the first place. exodus is not a new concept. read history. recent history, if you are too lazy to do research. think israel. think revolution. think china. think cuba. think russia. think america. think evolution if revolution scares you. think of building a new land and living in it, free at last, free at last, thank god almighty…

did you know, for instance, that liberia will grant you a passport if you ask for one? they used to offer free land too but i don't know if that is still true. i am not saying that it will be easy. it will probably be hell for awhile but we need to do it if we are going to survive. we need a strong homeland. we don't all have to live there, once it is a reality, anymore than all chinese have to live in china. they have a homeland that is strong and that makes them strong in the world.

we need backup and a safe haven. we need an army and a navy and an air force and marines who have a reputation for kicking ass and taking names. we need our own banks and schools and television networks and satellites and hospitals and credit rating systems and insurance companies and laws and courts and passports and everything else. we need to find our africanness and join with our brothers and sisters there and we need to trade with the world as equals.

we can once again welcome strangers from other lands to live in peace and prosperity among us, this time keeping an eye on the future. we have never been a xenophobic people and there is no reason to change that. racism has never been our way.

think about what is going on in america. fascism is on the rise. we are on the descent. our children will not make it unless we do something drastic. we don't have to leave empty handed either. think of moses and old pharaoh, since you have a passing familiarity with the bible stories. think of israel today and all the money that is given in aid. why not us too? lord knows, we are owed big time. i don't seem to remember too many of us getting our forty acres nor our mules, do you? think of the interest on that one alone. ha. think of the interest on that one alone.

let's be very clear about this…

george bush was not the problem. the gop is not the problem. the dnc are not our saviors. there is no difference between the republicans and the democrats except the democrats talk kinder and have better personalities and haircuts. then they get into office and do exactly the same shit the republicans do. there is no democracy. voting is a sham even though you fought and died for the right. you used to get to go into a booth and pick the lesser of two evils and now even that is not true. you can thank electronic voting for that. politics is an illusion, it is not real. it appears to be a life and death struggle but that is just to keep you occupied and entertained and distracted and to keep you dreaming and hoping while slaving for the benefit of people with too much already. less than one thousand families control the vast majority of the wealth in america, i've read.

we all labor for them in one way or another. they pay us a pittance for toiling our lives away every day and then figure out slick ways to get it all back and then some. they own the banks which finance our homes and cars and credit cards. they make the cars, they make the homes, they make the credit cards and set all the rates of interest; they make the rules.

both sides of the political spectrum are financed and ruled by the moneyed class; the super rich. the same folks who own everything run everything. the uber rich are too rich and getting richer. the poor poor are too poor and getting poorer. the system itself is the problem. america needs a revolution and it will get a revolution, sooner or later. hell, the military is ready to overthrow the government right now but that does not spell relief for you and me, brother. since when are we looking to the right wing military establishment or to the cia, for god's sake, for salvation? and the militias? the timothy mcvee's and the rest of his well armed brethren plotting away in the private and secret mountain redoubts of america are seriously ready to take it to the streets but what happens to you and me should they win? they are not our friends. they are kissing cousins to the kkk, folks. ditto the tea party, by the way.

the conflict that is brewing is not our business unless we, once again, decide to fight for america only to suffer, once again, when the fighting is over and the victorious take their laps and make their changes. i say, let's not do it this time. let's go about our own, long, long overdue business and leave this to the white folks and the mexicans. the mexicans may have a dog in this fight because so much of this land was stolen from them over the years but we don't unless we are so brain-washed that we cannot think and go for ourselves. it is a matter of the adult responsibility and the decision making process that a free people will engage in from time to time as the need arises, you dig? check history. recent history, if you are too lazy to do serious research. despite your misgivings, there is really nothing all that revolutionary about what i am saying. it is just plain old common sense and long overdue, at that.

killer katrina showed us the truth; bless her twirling skirts and overflowing waters. are you too blind to see it? think about it. that is all i ask. just think about it.

One4DeBrovahs

MIND

boston, outside in

boston needs a good old fashioned riot. i hate to say it but it is what i think.

now don't get me wrong, i am not advocating violence, exactly…

what i mean is that a riot serves a useful purpose in a big picture, clearing the air, kind of way.

take los angeles, where i'm from, for example. every few years or maybe it's every decade or so, the colored folks there just sort of loose their minds for a few days and let loose the rage they feel for being trapped in an unfair situation. the catalyst is usually some outrage like the rodney king beating or, more specifically, the fact that the cops who whooped upside his head so vigorously got off because the trial was moved to an all white suburb and, by sheer coincidence, a place of residence for many of those same cops, a place called simi valley and the good citizens there found that the policemen were merely doing their jobs to beat a black man senseless and to within an inch of his life for being a drunken fool and a bad driver to boot and even found it defensible that when brother rodney rose from the ground in a super human effort, trying to run for his life, pushing a policeman out of his way so he could escape the killing blows and was obviously in shock and operating on the pure animal instinct of just trying to survive no matter what, that even that action represented a move of aggression on his part and justified further ass-whoopery. yes, that is what they found, as incredible as it seems now, in the hindsight telling and without the artifice of a court system that allows lies to pass for logical argument if told with enough of a straight face, as long as those lies support the status quo of racism and bigotry and brutality that is the norm and always has been when it comes to the never ending war on black men in america.

the result of that latest outrage and outrage it was because those vicious thugs were as guilty as guilty can be and only got off because they were judged by a jury of their peers, their real redneck peers and rednecks have their own sense of frontier justice and what the cops did to brother rod fit right in with it, much the same as our reaction to oj and his alleged murderous rampage was one of little real care, since it seemed about time that some brother somewhere got away with murdering some white folks and it did not matter who got it and it still doesn't, sorry to have to break it to you, it still doesn't matter at all and we occasionally get a chuckle out of it because white folks can't seem to get over it, was that there was a price to be paid. the funniest part of the whole oj thing was that he was their nigger, not ours and for him to supposedly go all ballistic and shit and kill the hell out of those two trashy foolish people completely surprised his betters. they thought that old oj had forgotten how to be a free black man, they thought he was tame. they forgot that he was from mean, mean oakland and that he had made his money and fame in the violent world of football and had done so by being tougher and faster and stronger and more ruthless than his competition and that he had broken jim brown's records and jim brown makes no bones about how savage he is, in fact he revels in it and they were surprised to learn that there might be an african warrior hiding behind oj's eyes too, just like with jim's eyes and they were surprised to realize that he might have been just pretending, just playing the game and was not at all the house servant that they loved to call uncle. they were surprised to come to the sudden realization that maybe he was beating the white man at his own game, just like so many of us gently do. we usually travel under the radar, light footed and quiet or we are so quick that by the time we have performed our hit and run, to get whatever it is that we want, they are left wondering what got them because as they lift their battered heads from the dust we are so far away into the horizon that they cannot identify the tags of the truck that just ran them down. maybe oj just proved that he had a little more metal than they thought and was not quite as stupid as he appeared. the whole mess cost him time and money but he didn't seem to care about it much nor about his reputation and it made us chuckle, if anything at all. right on, brother oj, right on.

at any rate, in the case of brother rod and the policemen, when the verdict was handed down and the white men had their little celebratory moment when they thanked the jury for allowing justice to prevail and signaling once again that all you have to do is be white to be right and that black had better step back, even the black mayor of los angeles, old tom bradley himself, an ex-policeman with a mild mannered reputation as a politico but also a well earned reputation as a brutal policeman, stepped forward to express his own dismay.

the city erupted slowly. reginald denny was dragged from his truck and got his ass kicked for being silly enough to not just keep driving and avoid the urge to roll down his window to shout at the angry young black men milling about to get the fuck out of the street, you niggers. that is what he did and said and that is not part of the widely reported lore about the incident. he could not keep his mouth shut and his eyes on the fucking road because it was a white man's day; that was what the verdict declared.

the city erupted slowly. it was time to let loose the rage for a minute or two. time to loot and set fire to the latest economic invaders of the community and make no mistake about it; that is what it was. there were few houses burnt and few black owned businesses burned on purpose. there were some inadvertent victims but even the owners knew it was accidental, just bad luck.

one of the strangest proofs of that fact that i saw was a liquor store that was not far from my house. a liquor store that was owned by a japanese man survived the days of fire and anger just fine, in fact he stayed open and did a brisk business throughout. he had a hand-made sign taped outside on his store window saying that he was a soul brother too. the truth was that he had black employees for years to prove it and he lived not two or three blocks from his store in the hood and had lived there for years. everybody knew him and his wife and his kids. his kids went to dorsey or l.a. high and were among the japanese that were sometimes called buddha heads by us and who sometimes called us niggers to our faces, as we do all the time with each other; with no offense intended on either part.

someone should do a harvard study on the fact that the japanese and black populations of los angeles lived together in peace and harmony following the release of the japanese from the concentration camps of world war two. the japanese moved into our neighborhoods because they knew that they had nothing to fear from us. we were not racists and had had nothing to do with their unjust treatment, confinement and the theft of their lands and considerable wealth. the japanese moved in with their families and distinctive trees and gardens and we moved over to allow them space. their kids went to school with us and in some instances out-cooled the brothers and sisters. they had high pompadour hair and wore their pants pulled up half way to their chests just like pachukos, the latino gang bangers of the day. they had the slickest of the low-rider cars sometimes with the right sounds blasting as they slowly paraded along with everybody else in those days. they talked cool, they walked cool and they danced cool, just like us. the boys dated black and latino girls just as easily as they dated japanese girls and the girls dated brothers and latinos boys and nobody thought anything about it. and - they often married and had half black/half japanese, half latino/half japanese children who were loved and cherished by both sides of the families and still are to this day.

the key to mr. fugiyamma's store being spared the invader's fate was that he hired from the community and lived in the community and his being japanese and staying very japanese with all it's foreignness of food and language and sometimes his even being in a foul mood and not being afraid to show it meant little in the negative because a man has the right to be whoever he is if he is free and living among free people and that is how he did it. he treated everyone like fellow travelers and was given the same accord. his was not an isolated story either, it was the normal story. someone should do a harvard study.

no, the rage was reserved for the latest round of economic invaders; i think it was the koreans this time. they did not live in the community. they did not hire from the community. no one knew their wives or children. the money they made went to build their own korea town a few miles away. a korea town filled with signs in korean and businesses that did not welcome strangers of any race. they did not contribute to anything in the community except cheap goods at inflated prices. they did not smile at the children. they talked too loud and treated everyone who came into their shops like thieves. there had even been an incident where an elderly korean woman who spoke not a word of english shot and killed a little sister for stealing even though the 13 year old girl was approaching the cash register with money in her hand after putting a bottle of orange juice in her back pack at the refrigerator. the whole incident was caught on video tape. in the case of rodney and the cops, being caught on tape was not enough but for the poor and old korean woman, it was enough and she was convicted of some crime or another. the store was burnt to the ground by the neighborhood a few days later.

in earlier years, it had been jews who were the invaders and then it was the arabs. each time, they were run out, burned or looted and another immigrant group moved in to reap the benefit of black dollars, in a city full of black people. that there were few black owned businesses, far more than boston, to be sure, but not enough to make invaders feel they have serious competition is another matter entirely having a lot to do with red-lined bank loan policies and the entire credit system that holds many of us back and down. we all know about that one. they can say what they want to about it but we all know about that one. the white man is one tricky motherfucker but that doesn't mean we don't know what he is doing, it just means that we can't do anything about it most of the time. we still have to go to his courts and to his agency offices for relief of an injustice and we all know how that usually turns out. it is just the way it is and it has always been this way.

every now and again, though, he goes too far.

i remember the watts riots of my youth. it started over a routine stop gone wrong; a routine, driving while black traffic stop and apparently somebody made a wrong move and then somebody lay dead and all hell broke loose because the event happened too close to the victim's family at the nickerson gardens projects and they got a little upset when they found out about it.

i was too young to go out at night and my brother was too old to be kept in. he returned night after night with fresh booty, though he never revealed where he got it. i got a flimsy and cheap guitar that i thought was the greatest. he had watches, rings and lighters and all kinds of neat stuff. i think he must have gone into a pawn shop. i remember watching the national guard actually drive down our little, narrow street before they settled into the local grade school playground. the passing trucks of soldiers with machine guns at the ready were a sobering sight to most revelers but to me it was cool.

i had no fear because i was only a kid and they weren't aiming the guns at anybody and i was excited to see actual weapons like on combat or that my g.i joes had in miniature. i admit it; i played with g.i. joes all the way up to the ninth grade and finally threw them all away when i started high school. i remember thinking that i was too old for this stuff and had been for quite a while and was mildly ashamed that i still had them. needless to say, though, the riot cooled out not too long after that.

i remember the newscaster, george putnam, on tv showing his huge gun under his coat, like he thought wild negroes were coming after his redneck ass personally. the funny thing about it was that it was not really a race riot, in the literal sense, like they had in l.a. in the forties, when whites killed a bunch of mexicans or any of the other race riots from history, where whites went on a rampage and killed somebody or bodies darker than themselves for some reason or another. they have never really needed much of an excuse beyond being liquored and fired up about some rumored slight from some uppity so and so darky of some kind to get going.

i may be wrong but i am not aware of black people behaving that way generally. even silly reginald denny may have been seriously whomped on but those young brothers were not trying to kill him particularly. if he had died, it would have not bothered them, i admit it, but the fact that he did not die means that they were not seriously trying to kill him. he was helpless and alone and after the coup de gras with the toilet porcelain upside the head, they left him alone, hurt but very much alive. when he was rescued by people who lived near there and had seen it on tv (black people, by the way, that brother who used to be on bay watch and looks kind of like martin luther king was one of them) nobody interfered. i think there might have been one other incident where somebody got dragged out of their car and roughed up a little. once again, the crowd of black bystanders came to the rescue.

that is the thing with us. you have very little to fear from a group of black folks, even when we are excited. there is always someone in the crowd who will not go along with mindless butchery and makes the others ashamed. you might have to bear our praying loudly and longly or our singing melodiously and well or our marching down your street in an orderly fashion and holding banners or our frequent amening of the speakers who can get us excited by the beauty and power of their rhythmic rhetoric but you don't have to fear a rope and a tree branch. we are not big on setting folks on fire or castration or tearing somebody limb from limb or cutting babies from wombs or dragging folks from the backs of cars or any of the other things that excited whites get up to quite easily, it seems. them, you have to fear in groups 'cause they will seriously fuck you up in many terrible, terrible, unimaginably horrible ways. alone and outnumbered, there is nobody less likely to start trouble than a white man but a troubled or frightened or angry brother alone might just cut your head off before he is overwhelmed, outnumbered or not, ask o.j about that one. i suspect he might be able to explain it to you.

our riots are more like anarchistic shopping sprees. we just gotta have some new stuff. and - then we get rid of the parasites that plague us. we do so enjoy a good fire. we are not thinking about attacking beverly hills or any other communities full of those unlike ourselves. there was an added wrinkle to this last l.a. explosion though that is worth noting. the shopping bug infected more than just us. the latino population stocked up on huggies and pay less shoes and the yuppies stocked up on electronics. if you didn't see it, you should have.

there was a store called jay's cameras in the hollywood area and it was looted empty and the news crews were there filming and the breathless reporter reported that the parking lot was full of bmw's and mercedes and all the other late model toys of the yuppies and the guppies and they even caught a few of these happy shoppers on air, arms full of the latest camera equipment and they asked them why they were out and about on such a fine evening and the response was lop-sided grins and guilty glee and, yes, rodney king. there were other stores that carried computers and stereos and televisions and fur coats and diamond rings that suddenly were in need of new inventory and not a black or even latino face was within miles of the location when the shopping started.

yes, the whole city was sickened by the charade at the court. the endless playing of the tape showing how he was being beaten over and over and over again might have numbed the jury but it inflamed a city. everyone was sickened by the defense trying to make this barbaric act somehow the fault of poor drunk rodney. every blow was scrutinized to see if it fell within the limits of the law and the truth was that none of it was justified nor legal unless lynching is also legal.

the only ones cheering each blow kept quiet about it so we didn't know who they were but the police chief added to the confusion by boycotting protecting the city as the flames began at police headquarters itself. he pulled the police back from the streets to imaginary defensive lines for their own protection because he did not like the criticism his department of jackbooted thugs was getting, especially from his honor, the nigger mayor. the chief of police is the same fool who defended the use of the chokehold, even after it had killed many people, including my friend ray vitte, the actor, by saying that black people's necks were made different from white people's necks so it was not his fault that we broke so easily. when he started his pissing contest with the mayor, i think he forgot that tom bradley had worn the blue and had been as big a thug as the rest of them before he traded in his uniform for the silk ties and suits of the politician. old tom was not a bad man, don't get me wrong but he was not a weak man either, if pressed up against the wall, chaka zulu was right there behind his eyes too.

the city was in flames and many millions of dollars of goods changed hands involuntarily. there was little racial violence. that was not the point of it, you know. it was not about race. it was about control and the abuse of power. the entire city threw off the rules for a little while and just got jiggy with it. the wild, wild west was back and it was actually kind of fun. there was a celebratory feeling in the air.

a friend and i sat on the steps of the baldwin theatre and watched a group of suddenly free and angry people trying to get into the closed and local bank of america. it didn't work because the bank was tougher than it looked. we drank a few wine coolers given to us by a passing laughing crowd who had just emptied the shelves of a liquor store while the korean owner stood by and watched helplessly. everyone was very polite to him as they gently moved him out of the way. they did not burn him down because he was wise enough to remain pleasant himself. he looked sort of philosophical about the whole thing. i guess his insurance was paid up.

i didn't loot because i did not particularly want anything badly enough and i do try not to steal or lie and that didn't seem like a good enough excuse to go against my own grain. that's just me; i try to do the right thing even when no one is looking, fool though i may very well be.

there was something else that happened. in the letting go with rage and frustration, the city was on the way to healing itself, to righting the balance on its own. before the feds stepped in and brought federal charges against the officers because it was a case so clearly wrong in so many ways, the city was doing it itself. by everyone getting it out of their system, the anger, everyone was calmed down and we felt vindicated and that rodney had been honored if not celebrated. he was no hero, any more than o.j. was, don't misunderstand me; he was a fuck up. but - his very real suffering was acknowledged and the fires were lit in his name. he was toasted by us all that few days because he was owed that much at least.

and something else happened. lines were clearly drawn in the sand. you can be in charge, it was unsaid, but you can't go past this line. we will go along with the game, nobody wrote, but you can't cheat too much. we will follow the rules, was on the night air thick with the smell of smoke, but you better tread carefully. civilization is a mutual agreement all around. remember that, it was thought with every brick thrown through every window. everybody gets a little something or nobody gets nothin'. remember that too was added, with every blaze that was ignited.

the police chief was fired. a new and black police chief was brought in (from philly, wouldn't you know it where they had burned down a whole city block to kill some radical group of wild negroes a few years back with that very same brother in charge). i'll give him credit though; the police force was trained to behave more politely. in fact it was sort of creepy to have them smiling at you and speaking in civil tones full of sirs and ma'ams all of a sudden. they did not look at us in our cars as we passed them on the streets and driving while black seemed to be not against the law after all, after all and the tension slowly left our collective shoulders. they didn't mean it but it was happening anyway. then there was a little money loosed for economic development in the community and for a while things kind of looked up a little.

something else that is a permanent remnant of those days of heat and shouted carnage is that where i come from, we are not afraid of white people. they are, however, terrified of us. they have seen chaka zulu peering out from our normally guarded eyes. they have seen the wild indian peeking from normally docile mexican eyes. they have even seen the heroic and fearless viking lurking behind the facade and veneer of designer sunglasses and they have learned something important; that all white people are not with them and their viciousness; that some even remember the sixties and haight ashbury and the summers of love.

i watch the rednecks here in boston stomping around like the earth trembles when they walk because they have trust funds or good jobs or they have phd or dr. accompanying their names or their grandfathers or grandmothers came over on the fucking mayflower or whatever and i watch my people take it, accepting it like it's right. i have never seen so many hats in so many hands or so many ducked and humbled heads in all my life. they are the same everywhere, these rednecks, you know, whether they have a plug of tobacco in their jaw and spit into a can or paak their caah in fucking haavaad yaad. the boston brahman my ass. they are the same. the same selfishness, the same meanness, the same self proclaimed privilege. every now and again, i have to gently tell one of them that i am not from around here and that i would be very happy to demonstrate quite graphically what that might mean to their continued good health if they don't get the fuck out of my face with their privileged bullshit. you might try that sometime. the blinking look of surprise is quite priceless.

when you really get tired of it, for real i mean, you might also remind them of how many watts it takes to light up a whole city. just one if the watts in question is spelled with a capital w. it just takes one, if the wind is right. just one.

MIND

sedition

is it strange that i usually root for the other guy? as a small boy, my side was often the indian in the cowboy movies or the natives in the tarzan pictures. after all, i reasoned, these native people often had honor, courage, no guns to speak of or were seriously outgunned in any case and they generally looked somewhat like me and were being victimized in their own homes by rough, violent white men. the white men, who did not all have to be white, by the way, but were directed by or at the behest of white men and their interests in every case, could be dressed up in smart looking uniforms and salute each other crisply while standing at attention all shiny and polished or they could be wearing tall boots and big hats and sitting astride their trusty steeds with six guns and winchesters but they were usually still the aggressors in a never ending quest to quench their thirst for oil, gold, silver, land, bejeweled and ancient riches from lost kingdoms or women. rarely, if ever, were the white men defending home. they were always away in some exotic local, be it africa, india, china, australia, the south seas, south america or the vast grasslands of the midwest, anywhere but europe most of the time. even as a small boy, i could see that. when they were defending home, it was normally against other white men and i often found myself at odds as to who to root for because i did not really care who won unless i understood one side to be much more racist than the other, like the nazis. usually though, barring some other consideration i settled for the most bloodthirsty, since they seemed to be having the most fun and i had no personal stake in the outcome.

as i have grown into manhood, the picture has become even clearer. i have read about the history of this bloody land some of us call home. the examples of the unfair and unjust laws that allow thieves to cloak themselves in respectability are easy to find; manifest destiny being nothing more than justification to practice genocide against the red man as his lands were stolen, the slave trade nothing more than the crime of the kidnapping of human beings on a level that boggles the mind for the purpose of forcing a particular people to work beyond endurance. the entire population of african laborers in the caribbean had to be replaced every five years or so because they were being worked to death. worked to death. think about that for a minute. imagine it before you go on to the next thought. the asians tricked into coming here to work on the railroads and dying by the thousands because of the harsh conditions and inhuman labor required of them. our nation's history is full of these examples.

i know of the histories of other lands as well, so i am not excusing or romanticizing the pasts of other lands or peoples but i am talking about this country here and now, right now. we can get into the other lands and their histories at another time.

right now, this country is becoming the new nazi germany. our leaders are leading us into the realm of violence and aggression that marks the worst that man can offer and we as a nation are willingly going along like it is the right thing to do. some of us rail against it but for the most part, we go along, allowing our children to be used to attack a helpless enemy who is forced to draw upon the basic resources that all people have and that i have always admired, even as a small boy.

the iraqi fighters are brave, strong, fearless and smart. they fight when they must but mostly when and where they choose and they attack at will, relentlessly. they must love life as much as any other living and thinking creature, they are, after all human beings who love to eat, fuck, learn and laugh like anybody else anywhere else, yet they strap on bombs and walk among their enemies and their enemies' collaborators and strike at the will and the very hearts of these would be empire builders. not a day goes by when a suicide bomber doesn't exact a heavy toll in an instant. it is getting worse, not better, by the day. according to the media and the pentagon, there are very few of these fighters, these heroes, yes, heroes and they are fighting the massive and all powerful military machine of the usa to a standstill. in fact, by most fair reckoning, they are winning out there in the desert and in the mazes that make up the cities of baghdad, fallujah and of other points of temporary contention. i say temporary because the usa lacks the manpower to hold anything for long. they can chase the freedom fighters from a concentrated stronghold but they cannot hold it. as soon as they move on to the next target, the next point on a map to be bombed back into the stone age, the rebels return in strength and with no fear. they sacrifice themselves and their families to the liberation struggle that they have committed themselves to waging. the war of the flea; white men may have learned nothing from algeria and vietnam, but the warriors of iraq have, to be sure, they have. they have read their history and are fighting accordingly. they fight the only way they can. and they will win and they know it and they will not stop until they do.

i have heard it said that one man's freedom fighter is another man's terrorist and i believe it to be true. currently, i find myself living in boston and the city abounds with symbols, statues, plaques, historical sites and stories from the revolutionary beginning of this country and from the later civil war. the boston tea party happened here, white men dressed up to look like "wild indians" dumped tea into the boston harbor to protest unfair taxation or whatever was their beef with king george at the time. if i seem a little blasé about the whole thing it is because i know that many of these great white fathers were slaveholders too. the hypocrisy of the moment is not lost on me, sorry. beyond the narrow confines of my jaundiced viewpoint, though, the courageous fighters and deep thinkers of the american revolution are greatly celebrated here. there is even a monument to the black regiment that marched from here to fight in the civil war. but depending upon which side you were on at the time, these were either heroes or terrorists. i am pretty sure the english have very few statues celebrating paul revere, george washington, patrick henry and the rest of those brave souls who risked it all for their cause.

so, is it so strange that i might have feelings of admiration for the fighters in iraq? i have been educated to celebrate freedom fighters, even if they have not been fighting for my freedom and i can't claim to have a real problem with understanding their perspective. everybody wants to be free, right? it is a common human goal, right? or, by the same token, that i would volunteer to be the indian when i played the cowboy and indian game as a child? i was most bloodthirsty, by the way. i was after scalps to hang from my lodge pole and used stealth to get more than a few. i had a bad reputation among my friends that i was proud of. similarly, i would always choose to be the african warrior who was after tarzan's pale ass in my imaginings and that i would prevail every time, thus proving that history is usually written by the winner since the looser is dead and gone or in no position to contribute their two cents worth.

i was blessed to be the youngest of three children born to very strong and intelligent parents who had separately reached the same conclusion; that they were as good as anybody, white or black and they lived that way and they raised their children with that thought in mind. we were probably the first generation of children to be so reared among black people since lynching and jim crow laws and far worse had dominated earlier times and had infused our people for the most part with a fear of standing up or out. i don't know where they got the strength but they did, both of them – god bless them - they did (that is a lie, i do know where they both got it but that is another story, for another day, so for now…) and they gave it to us, their children along with a love of reading and thinking and an absolutely fearless way of looking at and questioning and challenging the world.

i was particularly blessed, says i, because i not only had parents who were wide awake and strong but i also had an older brother and sister who were making strides that i could follow. they talked to me and shared their worlds with me as they made their own discoveries. i did not have to stumble quite as much as they did because their recent paths were clearly laid out before me. i found my heroes through them, for the most part.

and blessed because i was a child growing up during the civil rights era, a time when we were re-writing our history ourselves on a daily basis because, unlike most losers, we were alive and kicking and some of us still able to think and reason our way forward. i was the recipient of an entire movement to recapture our lost humanity and dignity. i came of age during the sixties, the era of the black power movement when it was the norm to reach beyond the white version of things being taught, still even today this is true, in the schools and universities we all attended and where we had had our implied inferiority pushed into our faces every single day. i reached beyond all of that and read the subversive versions of history where we all had our moments in the sun, sometimes long moments that gave the world everything upon which to build and in knowing another version, a truer version, it gave to us that which allowed us to raise our heads proudly after centuries in the dust. subversive histories found in black book stores and the like, where often a book was merely copied on plain paper and stapled together because the original was no longer in print and the author dead for having written it in the first place (like walter rodney) and sold under the table for five dollars if you asked the right person in the right tone of voice. books that we traded like baseball cards amongst ourselves, within which brave scholars discussed the origin of things and how we got from there to here, wherever here was now. i reached and i learned about the triumphs of my people and of our struggles, our heart-breaking, soul and mind shattering struggles. i reached and learned about the struggles of other people who came to this land for various reasons or who lived here first and were ground into the dirt during the formation of what we now call the usa. that part was particularly galling since we have the nerve to have a holiday of thanksgiving to honor the original inhabitants of this land and to mark with gratitude how they saved the first straggley group of settlers, sharing with them and helping them make it through their first few winters here. talk about a serious mistake.

i watched all of the strides forward come to pass and i watched the powers that be terrorize, jail or murder every leader of consequence for the crime of thinking and acting like a free people on the rise. the killing of malcolm, martin and all the martyred rest did not kill the blaze in my heart. all of the incarcerated or marginalized or bought off did not stop the thoughts and dreams of freedom and equality. the fire may have been dimmed a little with each serious blow but it has never gone out. if anything, the rage and the flame have hardened and intensified, like a red-hot coal and it provides me the energy to fight on in my way, as so many of us continue to do and it only waits for the day to join in with others to explode into an inferno that will burn my enemy down, at long last. i still privately lust for scalps on my lodge pole, even after all these years if i have a choice of sides to play on.

so now we have a new war front to watch, in the never-ending battle for supremacy that seems to be the main occupation of those who think like that. once they have all the water and food and money and power that can be squeezed from whoever is closest at hand, their eyes invariably go to the horizons yet to be conquered and they get busy. it happens over and over. they get busy.

in my youth, it was vietnam and i avoided serving there by writing a letter that took me almost six months to compose. i wrote to the draft board that i was not interested in helping white men murder people of color for whatever was the current reason. i wrote about history. i wrote about the real reason they were so interested in this far off piece of the world. naturally there was something there that the white man wanted and in this case it had to do with minerals and ore, tungsten being the main one in abundance, if i remember correctly. i wrote about crispus attucks and his being the first to give his life for the american revolution and i wrote about the brothers in the civil war who fought fearlessly and i wrote about the buffalo soldiers who helped subdue the red man out west and i wrote about the black men who fought in every war and then came home to be lynched and discriminated against. i wrote about the reasons why we fought and, in my opinion, the reasons why we should not have fought. i wrote about my grandfather who was in the navy for over thirty years and fought in two wars. i wrote about my father who was briefly one of the tuskegee fliers and then i wrote about myself and how i was not going to run to canada or refuse to be inducted, since i could not claim to be non-violent, though i did not want to murder anybody if i could help it. i wrote that i would not fight for america even if the viet cong were landing at santa monica beach not ten miles as the crow flies from my house. i wrote that i would meet the invading army and show them where rich white folks lived since i knew that was whom their beef was with. i wrote to them that i might fight if the viet cong expressed a desire to come to my house and kill my family or me but barring that, the only real fight i was willing to participate in was the one that would ensue when the draft board folks came to my house to take me. that was a fight i was willing to engage in and i knew i would loose. but, i wrote, i would not go to jail, like my brother's friend who served five hard years rather than go to vietnam, if they insisted i would go. no, i wrote, i would go if they insisted that i go. i would go and would do my level best to be the best recruit in boot camp. i wrote that i would try to break any and all records for achievement at said boot camp, wanting to be ready and a lean, mean, killing machine. i wrote that i would also like to learn to do something useful, like how to fly a helicopter or something like that because as soon as i hit vietnam, at the first opportunity, i was going to go over to the other side and become known as the black viet cong. i wrote that if i were going to kill somebody, i would prefer to kill my actual enemy and not the enemy of my enemy, if it was all the same to them.

no, i wrote to them, i did not have any desire whatsoever to fight anybody at all really or to wake up screaming in the night like my neighbor who had just returned from there a year before or to end up in the veteran's hospital like him after killing somebody way too easily in a bar room confrontation that would have normally ended in bruised knuckles at the worst before he learned over there that killing was relatively easy, especially if one had a gun and the other party did not and to never be afraid to pull the trigger and he had learned that lesson the hard way, never to go out unarmed after being shot several times over there so he vowed that he would always be the one with the gun and to never hesitate because you never knew who had what intentions or abilities, little kids, women, old folks, grown men hiding in the jungle or just standing in his face at a bar, all being the same to him since he was trying his best to stay alive and to get back home from over there when his throat was partially cut by a prostitute of no more than thirteen or fourteen while he slept off the effects of spending time with her, that and the good heroin he had taken to shooting up over there whenever he could, which was all the time since it was cheap and powerful and readily available and it took the edge off nicely, the edge that comes from being in danger of loosing one's life because you are somewhere where you are the enemy to most of the population, right before he broke her neck with his bare hands and then dragged himself back to the base for help, blood seeping through her rag of a dress that he wrapped around his ruined throat, no, i wrote, i did not have any desire to end up like him, whose funeral i had just attended right after he was discharged from the veteran's hospital six months later, generously declared ready to return to society, for real this time, and straightaway he overdosed on the heroin that he had grown to need to see him through the worst of it, the memories, no, i wrote, i did not want to end up like that under any circumstances, if i could help it and, i wrote, i could help it. this lost and beautiful young man who had patiently taught me to play basketball day after day in the hot california sun, laughing at me some and both of us having fun doing it most of the time some years before he went away to serve his country. i wrote, that if i was going to go into harms way, i would do so on my own terms and die, if i had to die, at least like a hero in my own mind, fighting my true enemy and taking those longed for scalps to hang on my lodge pole. i actually wrote this to the us government. the passion of youth is something else, right?

i was seventeen, my draft number was in the low twenties and i was classified 1-a and i knew i was a goner no matter what. i sent the letter off and waited for a response. i wasn't sure what was going to be the result but i was sure it would not be good. after a few months, i got a response thanking me for my "informative missive" (their word, missive, the only time i have ever known that word to be used and directed at me) and that i was hereby re-classified 1-y. i looked it up in the book explaining the details about the draft that everybody got who was registered and 1-y (after 1-a, 1-b, 1-c, etc…) meant that they would take old people, crazy people, inmates, cripples, blind people, dogs and cats before they would bother me again. i would be contacted only in the case of a national emergency. i never heard from the draft board again. hmmm.

some of us are joiners. in my family, we were not particularly. i have tried to become part of organizations but usually, the organizations frighten me because there is so little original thought or even time to think. a path is set by somebody and off everybody goes, following the leader or leaders. i have trouble with that since i was raised to think for myself and have problems with surrendering to the degree necessary to be a good or useful follower. i am normally off to the side watching what the leaders do and see that it is far different from what they say.

i think that may be true for quite a few people who are wide-awake and thoughtful. it does not mean that we don't join in the struggle; it just means that we often find a way to fight in tandem to the organized struggle. we push the envelope and open doors on a personal level sometimes but we are well aware of the larger ramifications. i think my family has done that and i know i have tried to do my share.

back to now…

i read about the blood flowing in iraq and the growing numbers of body bags and secret flag draped caskets coming lonely home and i cannot help but silently tip my hat to those who are doing the sending. don't get me wrong, i celebrate no one's death. i feel for the families of those whose loved ones are in harm's way and get as choked up as anybody else when i see their handsome and young faces flashed across the television screen every now and again or printed on the pages of the local paper because it is a home town boy or girl who has died this time, but i cannot pretend to think that they are not getting what they deserve for allowing themselves to go along with the greed and murderous intentions of those who sent them, for being instruments of death and torture in the name of all that is wrong. is it not true that i was educated to admire anyone who will fight for his or her freedom? and - the iraqi fighters are doing that in splendid fashion. they are not wrong to fight us. we are wrong to be there and as long as that is true, i will cheer them on. not just for them but also for us, ultimately. we have all got to learn.

if it takes ten times more body bags before the american people wake up, then i say hurry up and kill them as fast as you can. this is being done in our name. we are not safe anywhere on earth because of it. how can we allow it to go on? i am in favor of all our young people getting the fuck out of dodge today but if it takes large funeral fires to make everyone else pay attention and react logically and not to have this knee-jerk reaction of saluting a flag and get to packing up body armor to send to our boys and girls over there without even forming the most basic question of why we should have to do so, after all, where is all that cash going if not to arm our troops even if they are in the wrong, they should be well protected, right? i am sad to say, if that is what is needed to catch our collective attention, then that is what we will get. it works that way. check history.

support the troops? think your way through the haze of intimidating propaganda for a minute. if there be justice in the world and the main perpetrators of these crimes against humanity be brought to justice, eventually, long after all the big shots have been charged, convicted and hung, it will come down to the same type of thing that befalls a lowly nazi guard found living in brooklyn or peabody or scranton or somewhere quiet and anonymous like that so many years later and is finally brought to justice by still grieving jews. every now and again, in this case, a us soldier will be found who committed a verifiable atrocity and some fractured iraqi survivor with a long memory and hollow eyes will step forward to point and accuse and testify that so and so sergeant/private/corporal did this or that in his village or house or by the side of the road and we will no more then accept the "i was just following orders" defense that the german soldiers tried at nuremberg than we did then. it did not wash in the post world war two trials and it won't wash now or in the future. there comes a time and place when a man or woman must decide for themselves what is right and what is wrong and behave accordingly. if you don't make the right choice, the time will come when you have to answer why not. in this life, in front of a jury of your peers or a military tribunal or in front of your maker later, does it matter? we all have the right and responsibility.

so, while we are still rightfully crying for the familiar sounding names and faces that will perish in the deserts of iraq and afghanistan, we would do ourselves and our loved ones a greater service that goes far beyond the chipper "support our troops" that is recommended as a remedy to our pain and worry, no, the greater and real service is to physically storm the white house and hang those lying, greedy, cold hearted, corrupt, warmongering assholes from the nearest high place and if such can't be found then drag them from the back of fast moving cars traveling in several directions at once and then bring our children and loved ones home from there. then demand our money back from halliburton and all the other war-profiteers gaining obscene spoils from the rape and plunder of another country. offer real aid to the iraqi and afghanistan peoples (read war reparations) and allow the un to step in to oversee the re-building of each country. release saddam from jail and if the iraqi people decide to hang his ass from the highest tree or to reinstate him as leader, it is not our call or our business. offer him asylum (in some other country, please, if such can be found) if you feel in anyway responsible since he is a creature of our own creation.

remember that we are in fact fighting in some exotic land and even though we are this time wearing uniforms and from time to time, get all spiffed up as we salute smartly and growl "huhah!!!" - or - whatever it is that soldiers yell and i can never understand since i was no soldier, as i have explained, we are still the aggressors here and now and we are killing literally tens of thousands of the people who live there and we are in fact stealing their oil and trying our best to defeat them to make them do what we want. remember that this is a rich man's war. fought on behalf of greedy, power hungry, cowardly sons of bitches who are hiding behind a flag or corporate seal and lies and purposely induced and constantly stoked national fear (just what color is the terror alert today?) to rob and pillage on a scale of almost unimaginable dimensions. they have already bankrupted america and have launched a plan to steal the natural resources from iraq, namely oil. never forget that.

now i ask you again, is it so strange that i often root for the other guy? besides being aware of the historical context of our times, besides knowing what i know and have now shared with you briefly, besides all of that and more: how can it be strange when i have been educated to admire people willing to fight for their freedom? some education sticks with a person for a long time, you know what i'm saying? and it cuts all kinds of ways.

One4DeBrovahs

MIND

sticks and stones

we have so many names for ourselves. it seems that every generation comes up with the appellation that defines and differentiates itself from the ones who came before it. for mine, we were black with a capital b with a fist held high and strong in the air. we were not negroes, we were not colored, we were not african americans, darkies, spooks, jigaboos, splibs, spades, octoroons or nubians, we were not any of the various names that have attached themselves to our hides over the years, both from within or without.

we were simple and direct and in that simplicity, that embracing of the name that was the ultimate insult to be hurled before knuckles got bruised when i was a kid growing up in south central los angeles where to be called black had caused many hard fought battles while playing the dozens. our blackness gave us a fierce pride and freedom and a defiance that was in the face of all that had come before. it was a throwing off of the mental chains of shame that had somehow become attached to our beautiful skin colors and we ceased to make distinctions between all the different shades we represented and we all embraced the collective black. we referred to each other as brother and sister and the men called each other blood, short for blood brother.

this was a special time, the 1950s and 60s. probably the most special time we had known since emancipation and reconstruction. this was the harlem renaissance writ large in the political, psychological and spiritual sense. all over the country, young and old, conservative and radical, religious and scientifically socialist, we were changing and studying and learning and growing and pushing and shouting and talking shit and working hard on a communal community level and loving every minute of it.

for my teen aged group and a little older than that, our clothes took on african colors and patterns. our hair was worn natural. short or long, we were proud of our kinks and naps and defied anyone to say that we were not beautiful. i have never seen black women look more beautiful than they did then. it is, to this day, my image of beauty for my sisters. soft haloes of thick hair or cut short and head hugging and to the point, it fit their features to a tee. hoop earrings, long necks and heads held high and the look of determination about their mouths with a sharp and informed tongue at the ready. they thought and talked and fought and led and served along side us and treated us like family, like brothers, like sons. they loved us passionately and were proud of us. we were their men and their warriors, fierce and clear and strong and we loved them back with all our hearts and souls and we were proud of their being warriors too.

but even then, in the midst of all this positivity, this veritable explosion of loving and celebratory self discovery, even while we burned the midnight oil reading about our african roots and the many roads traveled by our people since then, we never lost the use of the single most derogatory name for ourselves. we still uttered nigger on occasion. true that we redefined it and took the sting out of it but it was still there and waiting to be hurled in all its original harmful intent in a moment of heated anger. most of the time, though, it was used in a gently negative sense, as in "them niggers need to get their shit together" or "the thing i love/hate about niggers is the way they…" or sometimes it was used in the positively positive and loving sense as in your woman calling you a "pretty nigger" in bed, an endearment that meant no harm at all. black though we were and proud of it, niggers did not go away as they most certainly should have.

let's get it straight. it is a damning word with only one ugly meaning. it was meant to dehumanize and demean and it still is and the fact that we have given it other definitions is only a sign of our ignorance and lack of vocabulary, at its best. at its worst, it is a sign of how deep our self hatred has gone over the centuries of our sojourn away from ourselves. we have been defined by inhuman others who held us in bondage for their economic and spiritual benefit. our humanity has been stripped away from us and we have accepted it and made it part of our collective psyches. we know our name and behave accordingly all too often.

scratch us lightly and you will find it. the self loathing is not buried all that deep. the signs of it are all around us, from our straightened hair and bleached minds to our concept of even a good job. we sell our souls to the highest bidder and the bidding rarely goes all that high.

we celebrate who is getting paid and never question what they are getting paid to do. we see supermen and women striving mightily for entertainment value, like shaq or even oprah and we never hold them responsible to represent anything other than the most superficial images of black success. the money is enough and if they don't champion our causes in any significant way but get that big monty honty, the long green, then we are cool with it and wish we were just like them in their minks, mansions and solid gold cadillac cars.

we saw condoleezza rice acting as the handmaiden to the devil and we gave her a pass. she was not liked much but she was not widely condemned either. ditto brother powell who at least had the decency to be ashamed of himself after awhile. clarence thomas is going strong.

scratch us lightly and you will find that the self loathing is not very far away.

it has gotten worse as the years have passed, not better. today, all you have to do is turn on your radio and the word of self hate is spoken ten times a minute. rappers have broken through to the other side in terms of overkill. i can't listen to it because it jars my soul to feel the violence and self hatred so blatantly on display and the saddest part is that they don't get it, these talented young brothers and sisters; that they have been selectively chosen and encouraged away from any voice of true significance and they have infected our children with the same callous indifference.

not long ago, i was on a city bus going somewhere and there were two young brothers sitting right behind me. they were talking to one another and every other word out of their mouths was nigger and fuck, nigger and fuck. nigger this, fuck that, fuck this, nigger that and to make it worse, at the end of every sentence that was already laced with profanity was the term niggah used as a period. i watched the other people on the bus as they squirmed in their seats and flinched every few seconds. there were people of all races on that bus, all sexes and all ages. they kept their eyes looking forward because they were afraid of these young men and they only wanted to get to where they were going in one piece. finally, i turned around and said to the main offender, a young teen aged brother who was as big as me, big for his age but i have sons who are as big as me and i am not small and they are still my little boys no matter how big their asses get and i said to him, politely: "you should really find another word to use, young brother". he tried to stare me down and when he saw that it wasn't working he shrugged his shoulders and said: "it's just slang". i returned that i understood that, but that word, nigger, in particular was a very hurtful and ugly word and to throw it about so recklessly and frequently and loudly coupled with every other foul thing that was coming out of his mouth was making everybody on the bus uncomfortable and that it did something else that maybe he should be aware of and that was that it signaled to everyone within hearing that he had no respect for himself and therefore it was ok for them not to respect him either. while he was thinking about this, i told him that i was not trying to come down on him but since i was a little bit older than he was i was just trying to pull his coat to something he might not yet know. i smiled at him and his friend and turned back around. they continued to talk to each other but for the rest of the ride they talked quieter and did not curse or use the word nigger again. not once. i ran into this same young man on the street a few weeks later and he remembered me as i did him and i smiled at him again and asked him if he had thought about what i had said and he indicated that he had and then we shook hands on it. nice moment.

another time the same thing was happening on a bus and when i said something, the young man told me to turn around and mind my own fucking business and when i asked him what would happen if i did not and stood up and leaned in very close to him he started to say something else and i cut him off and told him that his friends were going to have to tell him about the next few minutes because i assured him that he would not have any memory of what i was about to do to him. he blinked and i told him that there is a big difference between a boy and a man and he was about to find out all about it. he glared but he said nothing else and then i went back to my seat. he continued to talk but he was shaken and as he got off the bus, i smiled and said have a nice day. i am ashamed to admit it but i would have slapped that boy into the middle of the next week if he had said something else that was disrespectful to me at that point. i was not being rude to him and i am not afraid of our children, i don't give a shit how dangerous they think they are. i am pretty dangerous my own self, you make me mad enough. i think i may have even said out loud that these were our children and if we did not love them enough to discipline them then we have only ourselves to blame if they turn out badly.

it was not a nice moment and, by the way, i think i agree with you that i need to stay off buses if i can help it before i either get killed or end up in jail. i hear you. i hear you.

just today, though, i was in the store down the street from my house and in before me were two young sisters with identical multi colored falls propped up in their hair the way young girls will often have the same sense of style and will do it together and one of them was buying something at the counter and she had her phone out and was doing that thing where you use it like a walkie - talkie and everybody can hear every word of your conversation even if they don't want to and whoever was on the line with her, another young woman by the sound of it, said : "fuck you, nigger" in response to something my sister with the multi colored fall had said and i looked up and the fact that we were in a store run by puerto ricans and there were puerto rican customers and an asian lady standing right there beside me and her and her girl friend and another older brother standing behind me did not even register on her face and she went on talking as if nothing out of the ordinary had occurred and her friend said it again : "fuck you, nigger" and then added for good measure: "you talkin' to me like i'm yo baby's daddy, fuck you nigger". and the young sister asked how her daughter was doing since this other person was apparently babysitting for her so she and her girl here could go and get their nails done, honey (i told you, you can hear both sides of the conversation even if you don't want to) and then she paid and left the store breezily on her way to get her nails together. these were two young girls talking to each other, not men, not truck driving, tattoo wearing, jail house swaggering men, two young girls no older than fifteen or sixteen and cute as buttons with their hair all done up and their minds on their nails next. i blinked as i thought about it and then i slowly remembered where i was and snapped out of it. i noticed that the faces of the other people were blank and careful not to offend and then i turned to the brother behind me and asked him if he could think of any other people on earth who regularly referred to themselves in such a hateful manner using such an ugly name. he couldn't think of any even though he opined that maybe this self hatred was also the reason we killed each other so easily. we smiled at each other sadly and then i smiled at the now embarrassed puerto rican woman behind the counter and paid my money so i could hat up out of there.

as i was walking home, i went through all the ugly names i had heard used for any people and i could think of none i had ever heard used by a member of that race or group, except maybe gay people. they might very well call each other a fag or a queen or even a dike with no harm intended but that was it.

to stay on point though, i have never heard a chinese person call another chinese person a chink. i have never heard a jew call another jew a kike or a hymie. i have never heard an arab call another arab a rag head, sand nigger or camel jockey. i have never heard a vietnamese call another vietnamese a gook or a slope. i have never heard a mexican call another mexican a wetback, a greaser or even a beaner. i have never even heard a japanese person call another japanese person or themselves a jap and that doesn't even sound so bad since it is apparently ok to call a jewish person a jew without it being offensive, i'm just saying. maybe they all do it and i have not heard it but i doubt that it is a regular feature of their lives and i can tell you without a doubt that they have all heard us call each other nigger time and again. there is no doubt about that one at all.

we spend a great deal of time and energy blaming the white man for our troubles. make no mistake about it, the white man is at the bottom of most of our troubles and he knows it. hell, they whipped us up and out of africa to build their new countries for them and along the way we were beaten and raped and killed and made the most ignorant people in the so-called civilized world. in order to hold us in bondage they first had to kill that spark of independence that any free person will have and they did do that quite well and then they educated us in the image that they needed us to have of ourselves, of our being worthless, shiftless and, yes, childlike niggers who were lucky we were rescued from our own savagery. they even used our own spirituality against us. we learned to love or fear the masters and our chains and we also learned to need them. even when the chains were removed, we sought to put them back on and to stay under the protective benevolence of our former masters. it is not an accident that there was really no place to go and we had no way to get there in any case. some of us tried and we were thwarted and cheated in broad daylight. most of our plans have always come to curiously unsuccessful endings and just out of sight we have been manipulated and tricked, over and over again. we have quietly blamed us for our failings and called ourselves by our rightful name. "niggers can't do shit right". we've all heard it and we all know it.

our leaders most often serve two masters and one of them ain't us. they have been privately rewarded to keep us compliant and orderly, even when we are striving. we are allowed to protest but not too much and not too loudly. because of the limitations that we place on ourselves, our protests don't lead to much in the way of change or real progress. we wax philosophical about our continuing loses and have been most patient and forgiving, cherishing small and hollow victories over the years. along the way we have learned many songs to sing for just about every occasion; indeed, we have lifted every voice.

it has been hard to shake that feeling of helplessness and hopelessness. god has sent messengers to give us courage and they have been slapped down. as of now, we are divided and disorganized and our children are killing each other over a hundred dollars worth of worthlessness or over territory they don't even own. our parents are terrified of their children. black women are being rewarded and moved on up, closer to the master and black men are on parole or in hell itself. petty criminals posing as pretend gangsters without real names are singing songs of gilded temptation and calling our women bitches, like the pimps they admire and crowing about the glory of dead presidents that they don't actually have in abundance. the so-called black middle class is trying desperately to escape to the suburbs rather than sticking around the hood and helping out.

the white man is to blame. we all know that but there is another side to that coin, my brothers and sisters. look in the mirror. you have choices, you can decide to be a victim or you can decide to be a volunteer. a victim is someone who has an unfortunate incident that is not of their design happen to them but a volunteer participates in the crime itself. if you are a victim, at least you can fight back or cry for help but when you are also the perpetrator, who do you fight and who do you call? we know right from wrong and we know our rightful name, yes? what do you call a person who feeds on his own young, who shits in her own bed, who spits into the wind?

we must heal ourselves, my loves. no one else cares because they see us not caring. we must break this cycle of tearing ourselves down with tools in our own hands. your mouth is under your control. your fist is under your control. your mind, which is indeed a terrible, terrible thing to waste, is under your control. find a new name for yourself and then treat your neighbor as you would have you yourself treated. there are words that heal and give light to us all. find them with your hearts and use them when you talk to each other and when you think about yourself.

it is not a harmless slang word, beloved. it is a hateful word with no other purpose than hurt and we must leave it behind us. as with so much else that is going on today to indicate next steps, we must leave the niggers behind and step forward into the future, free of this self hatred and loathing. we cannot call ourselves worthy in the eyes of the world if we heap garbage on our own heads.

sticks and stones may indeed break your bones but words, well…, words will undermine you.

MIND

race, race, racing

it's an artificial construct, you know. this subject or business of race, i mean.

sure we are people with different skin colors and all that but we are basically the same underneath the skin, is what i mean. the same dna defines us all. the same gravity holds us in place under the same sun on the same planet. we all bleed blood red. we all need sleep and healthy food and water and shelter and something useful to do with our rather limited time here together. and – we all need love.

now the business of race is another matter entirely. it is used, the same as religion or age or height or sex or sexual preference or political affiliation or profession or financial status or any number of other artificial barriers to keep us guessing and afraid or angry and confused or challenged and at each others throats.

through the centuries, race has been used to justify every atrocity and religions have been manipulated to reflect that even god is on the case. i remember the bible story about how black folks were cursed and destined to be carriers of water and hewers of wood because some long ago brother named cain supposedly killed his own brother named abel in a fit of jealousy and that god placed a mark on cain after his crime of the first murder was discovered that somehow turned him black. how this was decided to have happened (the mark being to turn him black, i mean, since none of these folks could have possibly been white, given the part of the world it is supposed to have happened in and that was africa, by the way, where the garden of eden was supposed to have been and cain and abel were the children of adam and eve, just saying…) and how it was decided that we were conveniently the descendants of the guilty one has never been fully explained to me but i do seem to remember that the story was told by slaveholding ministers to help us to be happy with our lot in life. i can dig it. i also seem to remember that the ministers told this same stuff to the slaveholders too. while it might have soothed the troubled minds of the slaveholders, i doubt that many of those held in bondage gave it much credence.

i also remember the honorable elijah mohammed's explanation of the evil that is the presence of the white man being created in some kind of a devilish experiment. his explanation that europe meant that it should be roped off stuck in my head too. somehow, i doubt that europeans would agree, any more than enslaved africans had agreed with the ridiculous story supposedly from the bible.

we have the jews and the muslims looking with angry eyes at each other and religious leaders from both camps spare no amount of spit and energy condemning the other. let's not forget the holy war that is being fought by our christian right against the infidels and extremists of islam. in eastern europe, the serbs are fighting the croatians because of some religious issue or another. and the band plays on and on and on.

religion is not the only other divider either. politics can be a bear too. the english and the irish are at each other and at the heart of it is religion mixed with politics. every day brings a new conflict to light and another massacre is revealed. in africa, tribal affiliations, as well as religions cause no end of trouble.

politics is tearing america apart right now. on one side you have the fascists and on the other side the rest of us. perhaps for the first time in many decades the rest of us are in agreement, not that we don't have our differences too. our alliance is tenuous at best and will be torn asunder as soon as the status quo is restored, that being that the middle class feels that they have a chance to join the ranks of the rich and to hell with everyone else. that is the main source of the discontent for most americans, you know, that the rich are showing that they don't really care about the precious middle class. if the middle class still felt protected and secure in their white collar jobs, we would not hear a peep out of them, no matter how many third world countries we invaded or how many brown people were bombed back to the stone age. and as long as there is no draft and it is not their children being brought home in wheelchairs, stretchers and flag draped coffins, like vietnam to a small degree, since even then it was mostly the children of the poor and voiceless who were doing the hurting and the dying, but we did hear from them then because the small chance existed that one of theirs would be caught in the war's net, no, if this time they felt safe and sound, there would be no outcry or not much of one, anyway.

but, they are not safe and sound any longer and their voices join with us, the poor and the disenfranchised because we are all in danger. the surprising part of it is how many of the middle class identify with the fascists. hope always springs eternal, i guess. they still believe that they will eventually get to the ranks of the rich and super rich and don't want to spoil paradise.

it is funny how the race card is played too. for instance, it was the indians who were first enslaved in the americas based on their red skinned availability and sheer numbers but they proved ill suited for the task, mainly because the europeans were a diseased lot in comparison and the mere proximity of so many new germs proved fatal to the native americans, not to mention that they were essentially nomadic in nature and captivity and forced farming caused them to quickly and fatally wilt.

then it was the poor from europe as indentured servants and this didn't work out because though they worked hard, they expected to be freed eventually and they could not exactly be vilified for looking different or speaking differently since they didn't look all that different nor speak all that differently.

finally, someone hit upon the idea of using africans. they were a hardy breed, immune from most of the diseases of the europeans or at least when a european got a cold, so did the african and nothing worse, unlike the indian who could be wiped out by a simple european flu (a small fact that came in very handy later, by the way) and the africans had long ago established farming as a way of life, so the work was not all that foreign to them. they were cheap and plentiful. hell, there was a whole impossibly huge continent full of an endless supply of the energetic black bastards and in the beginning at least, a form of slavery already existing among the africans made it a rather easy matter of trade with a less sophisticated people. we all remember about the beads and manhattan island, yes? yes, a few beads and blankets and mirrors and firesticks could bring quite a return on investment when dealing with folks from other cultures who had not seen such treasures before or maybe had a different way of calculating value.

this is not to say that africans fared any better than the red man. they died by the millions. in the caribbean islands the entire population numbering five million or so of captured workers had to be replaced every five years because they died from overwork, neglect and brutality. the brutality part was because the africans did not take too well to their new reality and resisted mightily.

this says nothing of the millions upon millions who perished before they were ever put to work. killed in the capture or on the boat ride over or murdered because they were at the mercy of brutal men with lusts that had to be slaked. the sharks took to following the slave ships because it was worth their while so great was the bounty of the dead or those nearly so.

all in all, africa lost over 100 million in population during this four hundred year period. that is not the total lost to the slave trade; that is just how much the population was reduced on the continent itself over a four hundred year period. the birth rate actually declined so great was the destruction. now add in every death in the new world and you come to a total of several hundred million easily. it was and remains the single greatest crime the world has ever known. stalin was an amateur by comparison, the nazis mere children at play, poll pot a piker.

the race card was played over and over during this time to reduce the drag of guilt by declaring that these were savage animals because money was being made. europe was getting fat with the profits and america was being made strong in the world because of the billions, even trillions of dollars in trade that was the result of all this forced labor. the markets overflowed as the result of all this forced labor. besides, they had the mark of cain on them so this was as god ordained and the european was only doing his god's work. the color black became associated with inhuman labor and treatment because it was economically and emotionally sound to do so.

even the hardest hearts need soothing because they can still hear the cries of those who perish. the bleating of a slaughtered sheep can be heart rending because it sounds of a screaming woman. how much more so then, of even the soft whimpers and quiet sighs of those letting go flowing from fellow human beings? the heart knows even if the mind is telling lies. the germans became experts at the disposal of the children of david because the soldiers grew incapable of continued one on one killing. the jews had their ovens and slow starvations. the red man had his hospital blankets and tainted meats and sickened villages. the yellow man was used for atomic experimentation. we had the mark of cain on our brows, the jungle as our condemner and the ability of our captors to fool the inhuman ear into hearing nothing out of the ordinary.

racing paved the way. the recognized wisdom became that somehow a different skin signaled a different soul, a different worth. white skin was worth many tears. blond hair and blue eyes with a pleasing face and figure was worth a war. a jewish skin meant that you could take your time. a yellow skin meant that they did not feel pain the same as us. any shade of brown skin meant that it was just too bad that they were in the way. a black skin meant nothing at all, nothing at all.

how strange it all is. the divisions and distinctions have been drawn so carefully through the march of time and conquest and commerce. scientists have painstakingly listed the aberrations and peculiarities that set the scale from the lowest to highest order. and they are all lies, simply all a lie.

let's start at the beginning. the earliest of mankind has been found in the valley which is in the shadow of the mountain of the moon. that place is located in tanzania. all of us began there and spread out from there. over the eons, we went on foot in all directions. the egyptians built the sphinx to honor these early travelers, the twa or the pigmy as we know them today. they were also known as the god dancers because all they did was travel and dance for god. the egyptians knew them as the most holy of all people and the statue of a lion's body with the head representing the twa was to remind themselves to rise above their animal natures and to try to become as godly as the little divine dancers and the forefathers and mothers of all lands.

circumstances, natural selection and environment did the rest. in the lands of the burning sun people became dark. in the lands of the high mountains and glaciers, people became light. in the not so cold but not so warm and very windy regions of the east, people became light brown with tight eyes. period. end of story. at various times and places, all of these main types moved about, mixing and matching along the way and populated the other areas of the world and they changed a little here or there as part of the process of adaptation, evolution. but - they all began in the valley which is in the shadow of the mountain of the moon.

just the other day as i was making my way home again i heard african drumming. i was attracted instantly and wanted to find the source. i was with a beautiful and talented young sister named cassandra. she and i walked to a window and were delighted with the sight before us. there was an african dance class in progress. the sound of the drums was from about five or six drummers who had worked up a sweat and played in the trance-like regularity of rhythm and counter rhythm. the dancers were in full swing, hips gyrating, heads rotating, feet pounding, eyes closed and they were gone, gone, gone.

upon closer inspection we noticed something important. the dancers and the drummers were of all races and ages. there were sisters and brothers. there were white men and women. there were asians. there were latinos. they were straight and they were gay. they were all there and they were all cookin'. up and down the floor they danced. in the middle of one group was a shorter, middle aged white woman, not very pretty or special to look at but she could dance, baby, and after each executed step, she would roll her head this way and then that way and the look on her face, her eyes closed, was simply breathtakingly beautiful in its sensual commitment.

cassandra and i watched and were charmed. we laughed out loud and clapped our hands. we watched for more than a few minutes and then finally life called and we had to get going. i walked cassandra to dudley station and as i made my way home again, home again, i reflected that these people had discovered something and were demonstrating something essential for all of us to know. they were all dancing to their music, each and every one of them.

as black people we have a tendency to claim african history as our own exclusive territory, as a sort of talisman against what has been done to us. it is understandable because so much has been done to us. but this group of new god dancers sees beyond the illusions to the core, the truth. we are all africans. each and every one of us began in that valley so long ago and our lineage takes us all back there. we are all related and if we can only connect on that level, then we have to greet each other as brother and sister, mother and father, aunt and uncle and distant and long lost cousins.

the concept of race is a convenient lie that allows us to ignore each others pain and suffering because it is not happening to us, those others are different somehow, less than somehow. there is no race but the human race and we are all members. to realize it is to begin to create a one world where all are cared for and all are free. we are in fact our brother's keepers. the answer to cain's rhetorical question that was posed so long ago to a challenging god is yes; damned right, we are in fact our brother's keeper. now if that is true and i believe that it is, just how important are the other things that keep us apart?

the only other real distinction that has to be dealt with eventually is the divide between the haves and the have-nots, yes? but that is another subject entirely.

MIND

are they mad ?

let's use the following as a working definition for now: trying the same thing over and over again and expecting different results. that's a pretty safe way of detecting insanity.

imagine your neighbor believes he can fly. he talks about it all the time and finally, because no one is buying it, he decides to prove it. he troops up to the rooftop of a nearby second story building and before you can say boo, he runs at full speed and leaps as high into the air as he can, right off the roof. he begins to flap his arms and then gravity takes over and he plummets to earth, breaking his leg in the process.

now imagine him hospitalized and the cast and crutches. he heals slowly but finally one day, the cast is taken off and he promptly goes right up to the roof and does exactly the same thing again. same result. you see the same process of healing, same cast, same crutches. finally, when that cast is removed, you see him heading for the same building with the same look of determination gleaming in his eyes and you decide to tackle him and call for medical assistance. maybe he can take it but you cannot.

his continued belief in the idea of solo flight and his continued actions to prove it may consume him in a burning fire of inspiration forever until death but is also a sincere cause of worry for everyone else. we don't see it the way he sees it and that is putting it politely.

we can make jokes and describe him as being a few beers short of a six-pack or, maybe, we observe that his elevator does not go all the way to the top floor. whichever way we might discuss this troubled soul, we mean that he is insane. he is insane because he keeps trying to fly in the same failed manner. maybe we would think a little differently about the whole thing if he were making a few attempts to add to his method. a tiny helicopter blade on his beanie would be a small improvement. feathers. a rocket powered backpack. something, almost anything different would cause us to at least give him the benefit of the doubt. i am sure that some thought that the wright brothers were around the bend (another colorful expression to describe it, right?) until they succeeded and we would tend to take a wait and see attitude if our flight obsessed neighbor was on to something.

i heard my friends and complete strangers all mentioning that george bush was crazy. they said the same thing about cheney, rumsfield, wolfowitz and rove too. they said that they were out of their fucking minds, if you want to know the most widely used expression. i tended to agree most of the time, particularly with george bush. i thought it the first time i saw him when he was running for president the first time. he struck me as a sociopath at best and when i heard about how many people he was killing in texas, i thought he was probably a psychopath. i thought his brother was crazy too, if you want to know the truth of the matter. they just seemed to me to be really smug crazy people who had luckily managed to be born into a rich and powerful family and had, as a result, become governors. they were enjoying it way too much, especially the killing part.

but – that aside, i am asking if they are all mad. let's examine the evidence for a bit.

since stealing their way into the highest office of the land and gaining the keys to the treasury, they went from a half trillion-dollar surplus to a half trillion-dollar deficit in amazingly short order. they lost more jobs than they created and most of the jobs they created were in the lower paying sectors, while allowing the higher paying tech jobs to ship out to india and elsewhere on the globe. the number of americans living in poverty is on the rise. home foreclosures are at an all time high. they made it more difficult to get out from under crippling debt. they gave generous tax breaks to the super rich. they violated the constitution numerous times. they encouraged and introduced a right wing religious element into the political discourse. they introduced the annual month long vacation after being in office less than six months. they, through inattention, allowed the single greatest act of terrorism in the nation's history to take place on american soil. they introduced the patriot act, which is busily ushering in the age of big brother. they abandoned the kyoto treaty in favor of a freewheeling and polluting industrial base. they refused to sign on to the world court. they ignored the oversight authority of the senate. they allowed the president to treat the presidency as a part time job, his full time gig being cheerleading and fundraising. they spent millions in public money to raise the largest re-election war chest in history. they lied their way out of every single scandal. they lied their way into invading two sovereign nations and destabilizing the entire middle east. they overthrew the legally elected haitian government. they tried to do the same in venezuela. they created a birthing ground for terrorists in iraq and afghanistan. they allowed israel to commit continued genocide against the palestinians and gave them billions to spend on the task, while paying lip service to peace. they violated the geneva convention's rules for war. they created gulags and secret arrests, far from the governance of the courts. they marginalized the united nations. they boldly went before the world with fabricated evidence to justify their bloodlust and theft. they slimed all critics and risked national security to make a dangerous point to dissenters that opening one's mouth had serious and dangerous consequences. they awarded obscenely profitable contracts to the vice president's old employer, forgave continued fraudulent overcharging by same and allowed the vp to openly receive monies from his old employer, in amounts which were greater than his government salary. they invaded iraq with insufficient forces and had absolutely no plan to manage the aftermath of the invasion; the country is still in chaos. they allowed american forces to go into battle with less than state of the art equipment and armorless armored vehicles. they installed a puppet government and rigged the elections to place their man on top. in afghanistan, the american government installed leader, karzai, was formerly a vice president for an oil company and the only re-building they have accomplished so far is to repair the oil pipeline traversing the country. the only region they marginally control in afghanistan is the capital, kabul and the taliban is as strong as ever. poppies are again the main export and we are the main buyers. in iraq, the rule of law was not applied, with civilian contractors having the right to shoot to kill at the slightest provocation. billions in aid money is missing and hundreds of millions in oil revenue is missing. the war is costing much more than predicted; now topping the trillion dollar mark, with no end in sight.

on the home front, besides violating the constitution in declaring war from the steps of the white house instead of allowing congress the honor and killing wellstone when he refused to go along, they stole a second election with the help of black box voting machines owned and operated by republican supporters, who publicly vowed to do just that. in several instances, bush received thousands more votes than were cast or even registered in the districts and not a single investigation has been called for. using the same techniques, as a warm up i guess; they stole gains in the house and senate in the mid-term elections with popular politicians losing by incredible margins in districts that had sent them to washington for years. in three separate texas congressional districts, the incumbents lost by the exact same totals and percentages, the exact same totals and percentages. they created phony veteran groups to smear a legitimate hero of the vietnam war and questioned his patriotism because when he returned home, he correctly and finally questioned the validity of the war he had just fought so bravely. they created the largest percentage of citizens behind bars in the world. they gutted social programs and abandoned the schools. they were trying to gut social security and turn it over the wall street, even after the scandals that have destroyed the trustworthiness of wall street forever. they allowed enron and other electric companies to rape of california and then blamed the democrat governor and oversaw an overthrow of a duly elected official and managed to place a nazi's son at the helm. they lied on the cia, creating their own disinformation department when the cia would not manufacture false evidence fast enough and allowed the director, tenant, to fall on his sword to protect them from their own lies. they stifled scientific research into stem cell solutions and banished partial birth abortions. they waved the flag at every opportunity while pissing on and desecrating the constitution at every turn. they alienated their own allies around the world; even renaming french fries something called freedom fries. they held no press conferences that were not scripted and they co-opted the press in any case. they allowed shills into the white house pressroom to throw softballs to the press secretary every time it was needed. they lied repeatedly about any and everything, even when the truth would not have hurt them.

through it all, bush revealed himself to be ignorant, arrogant and lazy. cheney revealed himself to be an immoral thug and the power behind the curtain. rumsfield revealed himself to be totally dishonest. powell's reputation was in tatters and he was scraped off like shit on the sole of a shoe. rice was the bride of the devil. rove was evil personified and wolfowitz was his brother. have i forgotten anyone?

all of this is true and i am just skimming the surface of memory here. imagine if i did a little research. but – the question remains; were they mad? were they guilty of trying the same thing over and over again and expecting different results each time?

i remember a conversation i had with my sister a while ago. she was asking me how it was possible that the american people were falling for all these very obvious lies. i mean; it was pretty easy to see all of this as it was happening if you knew anything about the world. if you remembered the newspaper story from yesterday and applied it to today. to be completely honest, if you never trusted these people, it was pretty easy to see. you don't look in a magician's eyes, honey, no matter how compelling his stare; you watch his hands - you watch his hands.

that is the key to understanding what was going on. if you just watched the actions and didn't listen to the rhetoric that seemed to never stop coming out of the mouths of somebody in that administration, if you just looked at what they were doing as opposed to what they were saying, then you began to get a much clearer picture. in the silence that resulted from shutting your ears to the noise of liars, it is much easier to get to the bottom line here.

corporate raiders have hijacked america. you remember in the past few decades how we read of these business types who specialized in hostile takeovers of companies and then proceeded to break them apart and sell them to realize great financial rewards? they never cared a whit about the lives they were disrupting or jobs that were being lost. they cared about the bottom line; profit.

think about it for a bit, please. think back to george bush running for president the first time and how at one point he said that america needed to be run like a business? he was telling us but we were not hearing. he did not mean that the government needed to be run in a responsible manner, balancing the budget, for instance. he meant that as long as money was being made then everything else was secondary.

for sure, someone was making a great deal of money. you don't go from the surplus of the clinton administration and get to the record deficits of the bush administration without somebody making a serious killing. money does not evaporate. it does not just up and disappear. it goes from one resting place to another resting place, from one pocket to another pocket. you don't spend a trillion dollars (probably much more than that, if the true figures are ever known, which they won't be because of who is doing the counting, after all, you don't ask the wolf to count the sheep if you want to know how many are left, do you?) on a war of your own making without money being passed out like funny hats at a birthday party. you don't take over the oil industry in iraq and then just lose a billion or so of loose change from the revenues and yet that is exactly what they would have us believe. it just doesn't happen.

no, my brothers and sisters, they were and still are stealing everything that ain't nailed down, plain and simple. forget about frank and jessie james. forget about bonnie and clyde. forget about dillinger and machine gun kelly. forget about the brinks job of 19-whatever. just forget about it. pikers, one and all, when compared to the sheer scope of the robbery taking place. think about the fact that they looted the treasury and bankrupted the richest nation in the history of the world in broad daylight.

all of the smoke and mirrors of the war on terror, the war in afghanistan, the war in iraq, the pending war in iran, the pending conflagration in korea and eventually in china are only a diversion to the greatest theft in the history of the world. they began by stealing the white house, the senate and the congress and were given the keys to the treasure room and now the treasure is gone, all gone. they were borrowing at the rate of a billion dollars a day and stealing as much of that as they could manage without completely letting the lights and phone service be cut off for lack of any payment at all for far too long.

they were shifting laws to protect themselves and giving their friends and supporters fat checks for everything from soup to nuts at inflated prices with barely a light slap on the wrist when the stealing became so obvious that the bought and paid for press finally and timidly had to write a little bit about it. they were pro-business to a degree unheralded in modern times. the corruption was complete and totally out of control. they might as well have been carrying out the money in suitcases but they were slicker than that. they hid behind corporate logos and off shore accounts.

don't believe me? check out the carlyle group, as an example. check out who is who there. you will find names like bush and cheney and baker and other prominent and supposedly clean rich guys and then if you look a little deeper, you will discover that they are in the arms and oil businesses and dig even a little further and you will find that they own a major share of halliburton and that is just the tip of a very dirty iceberg. the government was awarding no bid contracts to companies that the families in power had a stake in. cheney, for one, owns millions of dollars worth of carlyle stock and carlyle owns billions of dollars of halliburton stock. ditto daddy bush. does it take a genius to smell the smell?

while they may in fact be mad (in that anybody who is trying to rule the entire world must at least be slightly delusional), they were obviously not stupid. the fact that they were trying the same things over and over again (lies, distractions, murder, mayhem, etc...) would definitely signal a troubled mind if it weren't working so well. the fact that their techniques continue even today to yield results can only be appreciated if you look beyond the rhetoric and see the results for what they are. a selected and protected somebody is getting seriously paid and most of us are getting seriously poorer.

mad? maybe. smart? absolutely. evil? certainly. winning? for now...

MIND

london bridge is falling down

strange times we are living in.

you have to admire the plucky english. bombs going off right and left and they seem to be taking it pretty much in stride. almost, anyway… as long as you don't mind a few glitches along the way, like the unfortunate fellow from brazil. the ordinary citizens are starting to get a little jumpy but the leaders are a different matter, altogether. the leaders are exhibiting that famous stiff upper lip that romanticizes the indomitable english fighting spirit. churchill would be proud.

of course, the comparison between the recent harrowing and horrible events to the comments of the leaders about those events creates a serious disconnect with reality that is almost too great to believe. frankly, it's rather comical and more than a little surreal. i mean, how can blair say that the bombings have nothing to do with recent english actions in iraq? how can he stand there and keep a straight face and say that? did anybody check to see if his fingers were crossed behind his back or something? has the boy been drinking or smoking crack? is the stress too much for him? i mean, really.

on the one hand, a prominent british think tank came out with a statement linking the terrorist acts with the english participation in the middle east debacle and on the other hand, the prime minister and others in his administration fired back that that conclusion was a ridiculous leap, absurd and untrue besides. it reminds me of that pathetic iraqi spokesman who made all of those belligerent statements regarding the ferocity and readiness of the iraqi armed forces prior to the shock and awe of the invasion by the coalition of the willing to be bribed and then his continued updates as to how the war was going and that the iraqi forces were prevailing. at first, he was an oddity and then, finally, he became rather amusing, after the fact. every now and again, some journalist fondly refers to him as baghdad bob, i think.

anyway, blair and all the other english leaders standing there, looking mystified that anyone would have the temerity to connect the events as a cause and effect sort of thing is along the same line. someday, we will review it and get a chuckle out of it. right now, of course, it is not funny but it does make one wonder just how far they can go before somebody packs them all off to the booby hatch. the british are not alone in this lunacy. our own vice president has repeatedly announced that the insurgency is in its last throes, despite rigorous and murderous evidence to the contrary. gw himself keeps talking about progress being made, to the background noise of the suicide bombers grisly work.

besides craziness, there is another pressure at work here. the english lion has fallen on hard times and their empire is no more. no more presence in india, the middle east or africa. no more streams of stolen riches flowing in as a result. i guess blair was trying to hitch his wagon to the rise of the new american empire. when you are second fiddle, you do get some of the crumbs. hell, even hitler had a few partners in crime, though, if he had won, i suspect el duce would have come to a bad end and the alliance between japan and germany would not have held, white men being what they are. and what they are is not being big on sharing, when you get right down to it.

still, to reap even a little of the vast booty of this latest heist, especially if it includes iran, syria and, eventually, saudi arabia, means that the cash will flow like, …like, …well, oil and that trumps quite a few misgivings. that is the ultimate prize here. one thing about being empire builders, or master thieves, you do have to plan the jobs on a rather grand scale, otherwise, the enormous costs and potential risks are too great to consider. i am not talking about personal risks or personal costs, since they have long ago figured out how to engage the poor to fight these battles and the middle class to pay for them and to do both without so much as a hiccup of protest.

most of the poor and middle class somehow have been bamboozled into thinking that they are fighting for a just reason and sacrificing for their own welfare and interests, as if the two classes have anything in common besides a close geographic proximity. trust me on this one; the poor and the middle class live in totally separate realities. all you have to do is to take a drive through the ghetto of any area and then continue on into the suburbs to see it for yourself. the grim hopelessness of the poor has no relation to the relative comfort and ease of the middle class. worrying about getting enough to eat and money to pay one's rent and how you are going to keep your children out of prison is a world away from worrying about how you can afford the skyrocketing cost of health insurance that is taken for granted as a right rather than a luxury and gas for your suv that is part of keeping up with the jones' and where you and your family will go for a much needed vacation this year. both have their challenges, to be sure, but they are not the same challenges.

it is a pretty neat trick to publicly present the same theft in several different ways and to snare the targeted audiences without them seeing the slight of hand. i guess we all hear what we want to hear and ignore the rest, like two men in church, one of whom is having an affair and the other is busy embezzling on a regular basis, will both hear the preacher read the ten commandments in different ways and will both come to the conclusion that somebody knows their guilty secret, but how? that's the question, how the hell does he know? often the reality is that the preacher is merely reading the ten commandments because he did not prepare a sermon for that week and is just killing time or maybe he is just fishing to see who bites.

to the poor, the military, with a capital m, is being presented as a way out, a way up. a real paying job now, free college later, free health and dental care now, a roof over one's head now, food now, clothing now, professional respect and advancements free from racial bias now (after all, look at colin powell and general sanchez), homeownership later under the g.i bill and perhaps entrance into the middle class later. who reads the small print that you have to be alive and kicking and in one piece to take advantage of the best parts of this incredible offer? who mentions that if you are among the unfortunate returning veterans who might be missing a limb or two or lacking your complete senses, you are on your fucking own, buster, you are on your fucking own. post war medical and financial help is sketchy at best. just ask the homeless veterans from vietnam and the first gulf war's post traumatic stress syndrome sufferers how they fared in that category.

but the military's marketing campaign is being directed at the young. what could be better, they are asked. they answer in their heart of hearts that to serve in the military is a big step away from the grinding poverty they all know intimately and a sure way to escape the streets and gangs and the prison cells and/or the early graves that wait patiently for each and every one of them. this is their probable fate and they know it and live it each day of their lives. these children know that the monster under the bed or in the closet is real and is always stalking them even by the supposedly safe light of day. forget the cause, in the larger sense, because that is way too complicated an issue for children barely able to read. better to focus on the personal immediate gain. be all that you can be, right now, right away, now. that and waving a flag that symbolizes all that is good about this country and whose meaning of grand sounding words like liberty and freedom has been drummed into their heads from their earliest memories. even if the parents are not buying it because they know better, they are not being asked their opinion and poverty has a way of undermining even the strongest parental authority. why listen to some looser with a drug or alcohol problem, who could not afford to buy them the latest brand of sneakers and that is why at the age of fourteen they committed whatever offense it was that caught the eye of the court system, the unforgiving court system or, if the parent is free of substance issues, spends all their time on their knees praying to jesus for a delivery that never comes? the come hither message is being directed at the naive and ignorant children of the poor and the parents have long ago been marginalized by circumstances far beyond their control, replaced by the bad advice of gangster rap and/or others of the same self-destructive yet conveniently celebrated ilk.

to the middle class, the war on terror (notice the difference in the brand name, a more sophisticated and comfortable audience requires a more specific, direct threat) is being presented as a solution to the worst fears of the parents, which by the way, are being revved up to fever pitch at every opportunity. and – the cost is only an abstraction. the military is voluntary and who would volunteer except the poor and the desperate? middle class children belong in school and that is where they are. they are not joining up in droves, not like in world war two or being drafted even a little, like in vietnam. no, their children are not at risk in any immediate, doing the front line fighting and dying kind of way. they are only being asked to foot the bill and that seems like a reasonable request when their whole way of life is at stake, to hear their betters tell it.

that is a secret of the middle class, you know; they always admire and listen to the sage advice coming from those above them, the rich and the powerful because they long to be just like them and are desperately searching for a way there most of the time and that also explains why it is always the middle class who get bilked out of their hard earned cash and life savings by every ponsie scheme or stock option fraud to come down the pike. you rarely, if ever hear about some super rich boob loosing it all to some slickster from wall street. and - no rich and successful person ever lost any money by writing an easy to read how-to-get-filthy-rich-like-me book even if the advice makes no sense whatsoever or is only possible to apply if you start out with a million or so in hard cash, usually left to them by some well heeled relative, to invest in your daring dream, like they did.

the singularly brilliant success of this particular strategy is illustrated by the fact that the middle class is being asked to and is agreeing to foot this bill without a similar sacrifice from the rich, who are getting huge tax breaks at the same time. the only explanation can be fear and desire. fear that the hordes of koran quoting, dynamite strapped, airplane hijacking ragheads are breathing down their collective necks and just waiting to strike at a café, movie theatre, mall, train station, airport terminal or school nearby coupled with the ages old lure of joining the ranks of the super and powerful upper crust - which of the two urges is by far the greater, so great that they don't want to fuck up being among the anointed before they can get there themselves.

they are willing to give the privileged few tax passes because it is their fervent hope to join them sooner or later, this generation or the next, and since it is going to be better than heaven when they do get there, why not allow it to get even better and better right now? one has got to think ahead in these matters. the rich have been working this one every since they were the rich and everybody else was only being held in place by theories, serfdom and slavery being out of favor momentarily.

speaking of the rich, they are getting much more out of this than tax breaks. they are getting richer and richer every day. the divide between them and us (whoever us is) is increasing by leaps and bounds. if you check the portfolios of the tycoon, you will see serious interests in companies like; boeing, trw, halliburton, at&t, remington, general foods, bayer, microsoft, etc... every time a bullet is fired in a conflict somewhere, every time a bomb is dropped, every time somebody needs medicine or anything vital to life, like even water to drink or food to eat, cha-ching, another sale is made. war is great for business. planes, ships, submarines, helicopters, tanks, jeeps, humvees, bombs, guns, grenades, bullets, armor, food, computers, communication equipment, medicine, uniforms, beer and nuts are expensive, especially when you are allowed to overcharge because you are partners with those who are in positions of power and nobody is really checking the figures too closely. war is great for business even when things are on the up and up but when the game is so obviously being rigged, like now, the sky is the limit. and - let us not forget the icing on the cake, as it were, all that delicious, thick, endless and oozing black gold, oil that is. let's not forget that little tidbit for one minute.

to the international community, this war or terror is being touted as a huge business opportunity. to divide the spoils of such an adventure is a plum too big to pass up. i am talking about both the coalition of the greedy and the other developed countries who refused to go along. both sides are complicit since one side is helping and the other is standing to one side while the crime is being committed. notice that there is no coalition against it rushing to the aid of the victim. the un is not sending in forces to fight the transgressors and to protect the innocent even though it is readily admitted that international laws are being broken. rather, the only complaint that the other developed nations are expressing is that they are being blocked out of the lucrative war and post war contracts.

blair and the english leaders are willing to put up with bombs going off and to transparently lie about the reasons because they are positioned to make out like bandits, if you'll excuse the pun. they no more care about the few folks that have to be sacrificed to continue this boondoggle than bush and his pals care about the people who perished in the world trade center, the soldiers getting blown apart in iraq or afghanistan or the folks who will perish in the next incident and there will be a next incident. you can count on that. the only question is when and where it will happen, never if.

white men continue to worship and believe in the absolute power of physical force and since they have the lock on weaponry, they assume that if enough force is applied, they can do what they want. the catch is that as long as they are fighting other white men, the rule holds because they are never interested in fighting to the death. rather like dogs, one will eventually bare its belly and give in. and - it does the winner no good to be dead either. the individual must live to prevail. they are brave as long as it does not include death. in order to enjoy the benefits of an endeavor such as iraq, you have to be alive.

the weakness in their figuring is exposed if the other side has a different understanding. where personal death is no big deal, as long as it brings death to the enemy along with it, the major threat and strength of the great war machine is nullified. the red men knew this, the yellow men knew this and now the muslim knows this. they will win because they are willing to make the ultimate sacrifice, over and over again. they will break the spirit of the invaders because the invaders fight for gain while the freedom fighters fight for a holy cause, one where death is sought as a badge of honor and there is always someone else to pick up the torch to carry it a few steps closer to the goal of liberation.

if bush and his helpers could use the ultimate weapon and still reap the rewards, it would be a simple matter to win the conflict but that is not the case here. it was easy to drop atomic weapons on japanese cities because nobody wanted anything from those cities later on. if they use them in iraq, how will they get the oil? not to mention that if the conflict ends too soon, all that money that is being drained away would stop flowing.

what is the total so far; something like 200 billion dollars and rising? that is a ton of money no matter how you add it up. i suspect that that is only the public cost being reported, the true cost being much, much higher.

no, london bridge will continue to fall. spain will see other attacks. egypt will suffer greater blasts. more innocents will be chased into subways and shot in the head. diplomats will be beheaded. private contractors will have their final pleading moments recorded for posterity. tears and blood will flow like the waters in a river.

all of this and much more will be our reality as long as the leaders, who are making the decisions, are about business first, the people second. as long as they are allowed to profit from their actions, they will continue to use the public military arm like a personal hit squad.

it is called fascism, by the way, and that is what we have going on today. look up the word. don't take my word for it. look up the word. it's what lincoln worried about, eisenhower too. does it worry you at all?

PART II. HEART

One4DeBrovahs

HEART

honey baby

i been thinking all day about something. it started this morning, when you were on your way out the door. you gave me a little kiss and a smile and then you were gone. the kiss tasted like coffee and omelette with feta cheese and spinach and onions and toast with honey, toothpaste and, of course, you. it's the you part that got me to thinking, see? your taste is pretty individual and i am sure that it is mixed up in my mind a little bit. i always think of apples with brown sugar and nutmeg and cinnamon. isn't that funny? now, it could be your hair that i am smelling and tasting since it is always in my face when you lean in for a hug or at night when you lay your head on my chest sometimes or when i smell your pillow when you aren't around. it could be your conditioner and shampoo or that special soap that you use. i never take baths unless i am sore or sick but the bathroom always smells so nice after you take one of yours. the air is hot and thick and it smells of fragrant oils and flowers. it could be that cream you use on your skin too, come to think of it. that's what i mean by my mind being possibly mixed up a little bit. there are so many smells and tastes that run through my mind when i think of you.

and there are the sounds too. your breathing as you fall asleep as it begins to deepen and catch in your throat just a touch. i know you don't like to talk about it but the sound of your snore in the quiet of the night and the way you always roll over onto your stomach and bury your head in the pillow so fast when i tell you to always makes me smile. it doesn't bother me, your snoring, because it's not like you're sawing logs or anything but it's rather a small and pleasant sound, sort of a quiet buzzing but i tell you to roll over because you always do it instantly and sometimes you mutter an apology like it is something to be embarrassed about. i touch your cheek and you fall back asleep. i like to watch you sleep or more exactly, i like to see the top of your head on the pillow with the rest of you curled up in a ball and under the covers and your face covered by your hair.

there are other sounds that you make. it seems that part of my existence is spent tracking your whereabouts. i can hear you in the kitchen by the clash of pots or the clink of glasses or by your footfalls in the hall or on the stairs. where ever i hear you, it always brings an added beat to my heart and a smile to my face because i know you are near. that you talk to me all the time is another bonus that has a double edge. not really. i am just kidding when i act like your talking is making me crazy. in truth i enjoy every syllable that falls from your lips, honey baby. even when you are put out with something stupid that i have done or said or thought or was about to think about i don't really mind that you want to talk to me about it. i am not used to all this conversation but i don't mind it.

there are other sounds that we will get to in a minute, in just a few minutes, ok? i am trying to stay focused here and if i go into that now, i may never get the other things i want to say said. i hope you understand. i assure you that i will not forget about those other sounds.

there is a bustle about you that disturbs the air sometimes. you move through a room with purpose, always on your way to do something or to go somewhere. i find myself relaxing when you are around and just staying out of the way because you don't need my help usually. like when you are cooking and every pot in the house has something in it and the things you put in the pots, herbs and spices from many lands and things i have never eaten before. you are leaping from here to there, adding this and that and making a mess and not caring at all. i don't cook that way, i try to clean as i go but your dishes are extravagant and deserve the mess left in their wake and mine are simple and probably don't even taste all that good even if you do eat what i cook with a gusto that i appreciate. i help you with the chopping sometimes and i like doing that. i have even learned to make a creative salad, something i never thought i would do. don't get me wrong, i like salad but you love salad and that is a very different animal entirely. i am always surprised by the menu and most of the time it is pleasantly so.

we go to the market on saturday morning. my job is the carry the ever heavier bags and to stand back. you buy parsley and mint and oregano and lemon grass and shit i don't know what it is and you are very serious about it and even ask my opinion like i actually have one. i can only try to look wise and knowing and nod my head most of the time because i have not a clue. you have this mysterious ability to decide what goes where in the house and most of the time i agree even though i don't necessarily know how you arrived at your decision. it's a woman thing and i can only bow to your superior wisdom.

that is the thing about a woman, she can easily reduce a man to a puddle of little boy quiet acceptance because she is so sure that she is right and that is in direct contrast to the fact that most men are faking it and have been faking it since the beginning. we don't really know all that much. we might know how to do our job but that's about it in the certainty department. for the rest, we mostly just tinker and get lucky. women are frequently wrong but they are never in doubt and that takes a level of confidence that is beyond me and so i tend to do what i am told.

the important thing for me is not to bring a frown to your brow. i cannot tell you how important your smile is to me. it is a gentle gift that lifts my soul every time you give it and i find myself tripping all over the place to get one every so often. a hug and a caress or a kiss from you is something to build a holiday around as far as i am concerned. your very presence in my life is enough for me to fall on my knees in gratitude because alone and unloved is so lonely and unlovable but the fact that you are also a good woman, a real woman, a gentle woman, a smart woman, a strong woman, a patient woman, a kind woman, a spiritual woman, a stylish and beautiful and sexy woman, well, that is reason for me to live on my knees in your presence and be happy about the servitude. this is true, you know. it sounds overstated and overblown but the gift of love is the gift of life and a woman brings that to a man.

a man desires a woman but a woman chooses. how you come to this is an unknown to us. we are men after all: brutish, loud, rude, selfish, foolish, rough and tough in all the silly ways. we can take a punch but if childbirth were left to men, there would be far fewer children and many, many virgins. a woman chooses the man she will take the chance on. they must see something in us that is workable or why bother at all? every man i know who is something beyond the ordinary has an extraordinary woman whispering in his ear. this is the simple truth. maybe it is our mother's voice we hear or our sister's advice or our grandmother or aunt who raised us but generally it is our woman who finishes the job. she knocks off the rough edges and teaches us to eat quietly and to talk quietly and to occasionally wear a tie and a dress up coat. she takes us to museums and shows and concerts and restaurants and cruises and long drives in the country and trips to foreign lands. it doesn't matter who is paying for this, it is the woman who takes us. it is all her idea. we would otherwise mostly be content to sit on the couch with the tube ablaze.

but, back to you, miz honey baby. i don't want you to get the idea that i think of you as some institution or statue. you are a goddess made soft flesh and warm blood and that is the wonder of it. you manage to do all that and still wiggle when you walk and make me pant like the dog that i am. it begins with the smells and sounds and moves on to the feel. a person who smells of flowers and sunshine or flowers and the ocean lit by a full moon or flowers and the desert at sundown or flowers and mountain air from time to time depending on the mood and the need is a magician, if you ask me. you do that and more. all the time, you do that and more.

you have secrets for me. things you say to me when we are alone or lean over and with your lips touching my ear tell me privately when we are not alone. you give me a pass to come close to you. i hear your breath and hear your sigh and rejoice when something i have done makes you cry out in passion. the sounds that come from deep inside of you are for me alone and i try to keep silent because i am shy but i can't because it is a duet, a song for two and i have my part to sing. i just can't help myself.

i touch you and feel the strength, the muscles moving beneath your velvet skin. your arms hold me tight and your thighs won't let me go. i am endlessly fascinated and excited by your breasts and nipples, under my fingers or tongue or teeth, lightly scraping. entering your body is to visit a shrine, i feel it so. to be allowed to be that close is an honor of trust that i am speechless to describe. to move with you in a complicated dance that leaves us both gasping for air is slow and sure torture of the sweetest variety, you know that. on a hot night, with the covers down at our feet and the sweat slowly drying and your hand on my chest or thigh, claiming me as yours is a perfect moment to be treasured and i always do treasure those moments as i calm. there is never anyplace i would rather be or anything i have to do besides lie there with you, sweet love.

anyway, this is what i have been thinking about all day, since that little bitty kiss so long ago this morning, my heart. it started there and has taken on a life of it own, building in intensity and complexity in my imagination and in my heart of hearts. i have been distracted and people have had to repeat whatever they have been saying to me because my mind has been elsewhere, you know what i'm saying, and they have also asked me why i was smiling so much. see? i been thinking about it all day long and i was wondering…, well…

if you're not too busy, that is…

do you think that you can spare a few moments for me to…

i promise not to stop until you beg me to…

then i will do it all over again…

i promise…

honey baby

One4DeBrovahs

HEART

the king is dead but not forgotten

almost twenty years ago…

five years had passed since his going over

a blink of the eye in time's eternal march

he lay in his box in the earth

out of time in the end

warm and secure and so cold and alone

the final place to rest and await

the awakening…

my father was leroy. literally, the king in french. no middle name, just leroy, the king. solder: to bring together and make stronger; a unifying element it says in the dictionary. check it out. surname a leftover from an ancestor who was a blacksmith and was called the solder man, renowned for his decorative way with metal and iron.

my father was one hell of a man, actually. he was very strong and smart and funny and talented and wise and he was kind to me. in my life he never so much as raised his voice, much less his hand to me. he worked hard and long and never complained about it, made light of it, as a matter of fact. he was a dreamer, like me and told me that we had that trait in common, me and him and his dad, robert the inventor, who also ran out of time in the end. dreamers most often do run out of time, you know, because there is always another dream to chase and so many of them don't work out.

i never knew my father as a presence in our home because they divorced when i was but a year old. i was the third child, born long after the others, the only one my mother told me was planned, to help them to come back together, to heal the wounds, she said. i guess i failed but i doubt it was my fault. too much pain and anger and too little forgiveness and understanding often drives us apart, yes? i remember the day he left. my brother and sister and i were in a bedroom and they were shouting and fighting out there somewhere in our little house that seemed so endlessly big to me at the time. he came into the room and kissed our crying faces and said: "i've got to go now. you kids be good. remember i love you." and then he was gone. it is my earliest memory of him and is almost as painful today as it was so many years ago and it is crystal clear in my memory after all these years. i was a baby and yet i remember his words exactly. strange isn't it?

i grew up with him on the periphery. sometimes, during the good years, it was weekend visits, every other sundays mostly. going to the movies and to disneyland and knott's berry farm and marine land and p.o.p. and to the zoo, riding on his shoulders all day long or holding his strong hand in the crowds. eating ice cream cones in the hot california sun. he never bought one for himself, he would wait for mine to start to melt down my arm and then he would wipe me with a napkin and then he would finish what i had not eaten for me, as a favor. it was a ritual between us. he was always using spit on his thumb to clean my dirty face. it was a ritual between us. we would usually eat dinner at his house on those visiting days and then he would read the funny papers to me and i would stand next to him on the couch and suck his earlobe while i listened. he never stopped me. it was a ritual between us.

he sang with a beautifully controlled, powerful baritone voice in harmony to the star spangled banner at ball games or other public events. he laughed really loud at the antics of mickey mouse and tom and jerry at the movie cartoons of those days and we would pull on his sleeve because people would be looking at us and he would shrug our embarrassment away and sing or laugh louder. he knew the funniest songs and taught them to us as we rode in the car. do you know catalina matalina? i do.

he sang silent night while playing his guitar for us one night at his house and i thought it was so beautiful and sad that i burst out crying when the final chord was played. he laughed at my jokes and answered my questions about everything. i still smile about his explanation of why two men were walking down the street holding hands looking very much like little richard and my following further questions regarding how a man could make love to another man and how, after he tried several times to explain the act using clinical terms that weren't getting through to me with my limited vocabulary, he finally looked at me in exasperation and said: "in his asshole, stupid". that certainly shut me up for the rest of that ride while i thought about the implications of that particular and most peculiar revelation.

he told me stories of my grandfather robert, a garvyite, a race man. he told me of his father's genius too. he told me after watching people jumping to their deaths in a horrible fire in boston, grandfather robert invented the hook and ladder fire truck, only to have the idea stolen from him by the ford motor company after he sent the plans in for consideration. he told of seeing his father's fire truck, made by ford, rounding a corner in chicago some years later and as they watched; it worked just as they planned. his father was overjoyed and kept laughing and clapping his hands as the details that existed only in his imagination unfolded. when my father argued that his idea was stolen and that there was the proof, his father considered for a second, no doubt tallying his chances of protest and considering the fact that a black man could not hold a patent at the time until finally he shrugged his shoulders and said: "don't worry about it precious, god sees" and he never mentioned it again.

he told us of his father entertaining the entire family most nights far better than the radio; singing and playing the guitar, banjo and harmonica while telling jokes and stories. besides his inventions, he was a master mechanic, a lay preacher, a poet, he made bath tub gin, he lost the hearing in one ear during a cave-in while working on the hoover dam and even acted in the silent movies in los angeles after he and his family had migrated west and how finally my father's father again entered a clinic for his tubercular lungs that had plagued him most of his life and had hospitalized him countless times over the years, one last time in california and did not survive the trip. he ran out of time. my father was fourteen years old.

he told of his brother then consciously sacrificing himself for the good of the family. he made my father study his school lessons faithfully. he told me of his older brother going out to steal food so they would not starve. he told me of how his brother was caught inside a closed store one night and was so badly beaten that he lost an eye.

he told me of his winning an improbable scholastic scholarship to ucla straight from jefferson high school's all black student body in the 1930's and why he couldn't go because there wasn't enough money in the scholarship to pay for room and board and clothes and books, what with his mother being a washer woman and all. how he, instead, went into the construction business and became an electrician and how he fought to join the union and how he had to fight on every job because somebody was always foolish enough to call him a nigger. he told me of the satisfaction he felt on the day that he walked onto a new job and saw his fellow workers, white men one and all, whispering to one another, passing the word about him and how one of them finally said: "hey roy. how you doing?" and thus began a new day. he had never lost the fights. he went on to become an electrical contractor.

he told me of how he had seen my mother in church one sunday when he as about seventeen and she was about ten and how he decided that she was going to be his wife then and there. he loved her from the first moment he saw her. he told me how he waited until she was older before he ever said a word to her and how he finally went to her house and introduced himself to my mother's father, henry allen, who was a thirty year navy man who drank and who would meet would be suitors for his lovely twin daughters at the front door with a loaded shotgun. when it was his turn to stare down the barrels, he glanced at the shotgun pointed at his face and calmly introduced himself to my mother's father and told him that he had first seen his daughter, jean, in church many years before and that he was there on his doorstep because it was his intention to marry her and that if he was going to shoot, now would be the time. he waited and while my grandfather thought this over with a few blinks, my future father stuck his fingers into the barrel of the gun and pushed it aside and walked past the startled man and called out: "jean, are you home? it's leroy come to call." and thus began the courtship. my father told me this story. my mother told me this story. my grandfather paw paw told me this story ruefully, sorry for having missed his chance.

they were married when he was twenty five and she was seventeen, over the objections of my grandfather and his mother, my great-grandmother nan naw, who called my father "that arrogant bostonian nigger" because of his even then direct manner and, sadly, because he was too african dark and my mother was almost white.

he told me of world war two and how he joined the air force when it looked like his time was near for drafting. he told me that he preferred riding in an airplane for a few exciting minutes to walking all over europe with a rifle, a helmet and a bull's eye on his heavy backpack. he took the tests and ended up in tuskegee as one of the airmen. my mother came with him. his irregularly beating heart kept him out of the pilot's seat and his superior mathematical skills landed him in the navigator/bombardier's position. he was to fly aboard the b-52.

he hated marching with a passion and regularly got out of step through inattention but he ended up leading his platoon in marches and reviews because after he had defeated every big man in the squad who came at him in group think punishment for their habitually low marks and lost liberties, they did not know what else to do. so, as he casually strolled along, they did too and when he got out of step, they would skip and catch up. however, he loved the songs they would sing as they marched or, in his case, strolled along and years later taught many of them to us on long car rides. i did not get the one about eskimo pie being mighty cold until i was much older.

that he never actually flew in a combat mission was due to the coincidence of receiving his wings on v-e day, the day the war was over in europe. the need was suddenly less severe for airmen and it was the only time he had volunteered for anything in the military, telling me later that he had observed that volunteering was a very good way to get yourself killed. he also told me that he had had plenty of time to reconsider the wisdom of hurtling thousands of feet above ground in a metal tube filled with lighter fluid. so, that same day, he turned in his wings, got his honorable discharge papers, stopped by the rooming house just long enough to grab my mother and then he hopped the next thing smoking out of town, back to california, leaving the keys in the still running car and the doors open just as it was at the train station for whoever wanted it or needed it next. his overriding thought was to get out of town before they changed their damned minds, the military being the military, thank you very much.

he was curiously silent on the time after the war, when my parents bought a house on the g.i. bill in a new housing development in a place called watts. my mother and sister have talked about it plenty. we always had a new car, a nice house and furniture, the first television on the block and a collie, just like lassie on tv. he even bought a new car just for my mother, a cute yellow convertible number. with my brother and sister he was gentle and a good father and a good provider for them all, my mother said. he planted trees in the backyard for each and gave them rides on the lawnmower.

and – they talked about how he was frustrated because of racism and disappointments and how he took it out on my mother until her love for him was gone. he was a tyrant and he was angry. he was violent. he beat her. the neighbors who came to visit would run home when they saw his car come around the corner, so acid was his tongue, calling them shiftless and lazy good for nothings. he was jealous of his pretty wife and he did not trust our handsome family doctor.

finally, tired of living in hell and knowing that she was worth more than that, she made her break and threw a pot of boiling spaghetti sauce at him one night. the years to follow were a succession of his being in and out of the picture. i grew up to tales of his brutality. but – at times he was a regular as clock work; every other sunday would see him at the front door that he had to knock on because he could not cross the threshold of the house he had bought. at other times he was absent for months or even years at a time because of the constant tensions about child support and simmering angers that could flare up in an instant.

these long absences would be broken by dramatic re-appearances, like the time he showed up at my junior high school and i was summoned to the office from class. he was standing there wearing his dusty work clothes and baseball cap. he spoke to me for a few minutes about nothing really, i think he gave me a book on the air force academy because he knew that i wanted to be a flier when i grew up and then he started to cry and he sank to his knees, took me in his arms and hugged me so tight i thought i was going to die and he kept telling me that he loved me, he loved me. he cried so hard he could barely speak and i cried too because i loved him so and missed him so and i was a tender child, a tender mostly fatherless boy who needed his daddy. every missed father and son game or event at school ripped the wound open again and again. my mother would come sometimes but it was not the same thing at all.

even though i was very familiar with the stories of horror that were shared like sacramental wine in my mother's house, i never stopped loving my father. i was not mad at him much because of it or afraid of him at all, like my brother and sister sometimes were. maybe because i was too young to remember the terror in our house in those last years they were together. he was soft with me, patient with me. he let me down sometimes and his absences hurt me deeply too. we built our own private resentments, one tear at a time. but - during the good periods he even took me to work with him sometimes during the summers and, small kid or not, he even paid me a good wage too, far more than i was worth certainly. he bought me a small tool belt with screw drivers and pliers and wire cutters and a small hammer hanging from a loop. i had a baseball cap like his. he taught me to install light switches and fixtures. he taught me to read blueprints. he would even hold me by my ankles high off the ground, over the side of a building as i installed fixtures upside down onto the buildings side to overlook a parking lot and i was totally unafraid because he was my father and he was never going to drop me. he was my hero, you know that.

somehow i separated the stories that i knew were true from my reality with him and finally, when i was just about grown, i asked my mother to stop with her negative comments about him. i told her that i was sorry for what had happened between them and that i was glad that she had saved herself. i also reminded her that he was my father and that i still loved him deeply. i told her that i would never listen to anybody talk about her like that either, no matter what and that included him. i loved them both. please allow me to love my own father without feeling that i am somehow betraying your love, i said. it caught her up short but she was not a stupid woman and she kissed me and we never spoke of it again. she never said another negative thing about him in my presence either and went so far as to say one day much later, when she was an old woman living with husband number six or seven, that if she had known back then what she knew now, they would still be together, that she was just too young and immature to deal with his anger, that he was actually a very gentle man who she could easily have handled now, after all this time and so much wisdom. it was a strange moment. she called him a pussycat, actually.

as i was getting older, he was changing, getting older too. he said he was tired of crawling under people's houses and sick of spiders and dirt. he became a lawyer at the age of fifty three. over the years, he had seen classmates, like l.a. mayor tom bradley, men he not only knew but also knew he was smarter than, get ahead in the real world, so he decided to finally pursue the education he had missed. it had taken him years of going to law school at night and then he took the bar exam five times before he passed it. he told me that when he finally passed, he had memorized so much of the material that he could simply pull up the book in his mind and mentally turn to the right section and read the answer directly from the page. he taught himself spanish and then italian and could not only play classical and flamingo guitar and sing, he also played the harmonica and piano.

the disappointments and hurts of my childhood stood like a wall between us at times. he was shy with me and i was sometimes cold with him. he had re-married long ago. his new wife was not a very nice person. he lived in beautiful houses and drove brand new cars as always. he lived in a series of all-white suburbs of los angeles. he bought and rode horses. he was the president of the local rotary club. he became a mormon. he was still defiant and was the angriest black man i knew in terms of white people and his way of fighting was to stick himself right up into their faces and dare them to do anything about it.

at one point he moved into a house that cost him almost a million dollars. his next door neighbor took exception to having a nigger as a neighbor and started surreptitiously throwing garbage into his backyard at darkness. my father puzzled about it for some while until he saw the garbage come flying over the fence one night and realized the origin and then he got the shotgun that he had bought when he and i were going to become hunters. a plan that lasted until we went to a meeting at a local hunting club and watched a film showing these brave hunters blasting away at helpless coyotes and we both felt more than a little disgusted and that ended that but he kept the beautifully tooled shotgun that he now collected as he went next door to visit. when his neighbor opened the door, my father placed the gun under the man's chin, encouraging him to stand on his tippy-toes for a bit and then he assured him that he understood how he felt and offered his own opinion that one of them needed to move right away before someone got hurt but that it was not going to be him, since he had just moved in and all. my dad then allowed the man to come down off his toes gently, never raising his voice at all and then he went on back home, to his brand new house.

he told me that after a few minutes the man came out with his wife and kids in tow and they got into the car and they tire screeched away. a few days later a moving van came and packed them all up and a for sale sign appeared. he never saw the neighbor again. he got along with his new neighbors just fine and, in fact, never had any other trouble at all along those lines. we laughed together over that one.

i got married finally and had two sons. my father was a proud grandfather but he started being inconsistent with them too. sometimes he was the doting grandfather, like the time he surprised my wife and me by dropping in, saying that he was passing on a nearby freeway and just wanted to see his newest and youngest grandson, baby cheo. cheo was in a playpen, next to the piano. my father went up to him and kissed him on his little head and made cooing sounds at him and then he started playing the piano and singing a silly song in spanish to him. little cheo smiled and laughed with delight. when he finished playing and singing with a flourish, he kissed cheo again, kissed my wife and then patted my shoulder and said that he had to run. he left in his wake a bit of confused but happy silence as we all pondered what had just happened.

at other times, he was strangely distant with my sons. it was getting worse and worse. he was gone for periods of time, just like when i was a boy. following a christmas when he finally showed up late with unwrapped and very cheap presents for his grandsons, i took him aside and told him that i would not allow him to hurt my sons as he had hurt me and that if he could not be a joy as a grandfather, a consistent joy, then to fuck off. i told him this. it was the only time in my life that i cursed at my father and i was trembling with emotion when i said it.

he went away. i did not really talk to him much after that. he came by one day as i was outside watering my lawn to tell me that he had left his jaguar to me in his will because he knew that i liked the car. i glanced at the car and then i told him that i would rather have him as a father and that he could keep his car, if it was all the same to him. he did not ask to come into the house and i did not invite him. he got in his car and left.

finally, one day he called me to tell me that he was going to have an operation. he was going to have his heart operated on, to replace the clogged arteries and valves of his heart with the healthy arteries and valves of a pig. i told him that it was a lucky thing that he had become a mormon and not a jew. we hung up on that one.

my sister called to tell me that i should come to the hospital where he had been operated on, that it didn't look good. i went and saw him. he was barely conscious and had bloody bandages covering his chest and a large tube in his throat and he focused on me briefly as i spoke to him, a small tear falling from his blinking eye. i told him that i loved him.

in the waiting room, the doctor came and told us what we could not see, that the operation was a success but that half of his heart had stopped working as a result of the shock of his chest being cut open. the doctor said that it was a miracle that he was still alive, that it was his sheer willpower that was keeping him living, that he was obviously a strong and determined man but that he would eventually tire and that he was going to die.

he lingered and fought the good and final fight for three days. i had gone home for the night and i got to the hospital early that next day and when i asked the nurse if i could go in to see my father, she said sure and opened the door for me. as i stepped behind the curtain into the area where he was abed, i was surprised to see my uncle robert holding my father's hand. he looked like a used up version of my father. there was silence until uncle robert looked at me with his one good eye and his one dead, milky eye and said: "i am just helping to him ease over to the other side". i looked at my father and realized that he was gone, that he was out of time. my uncle robert said:

"look what they did to my baby brother…" and started to pull back the bloody bandages covering his gaping chest, in order to show me something or other, i never knew what because i fled and don't really remember anything else.

my father's funeral was held in the mormon tabernacle near his home. it was a strange affair. half of the attending crowd was lily white and mormon and the other half was from my father's african american roots. the mormon choir sang in operatic style. the black folks just looked uncomfortable and confused by the lack of emotion that normally accompanies a death. he was buried in forest lawn.

there was some ugliness with our step mother over his suddenly missing will and we left her to it. i got nothing but a key chain that i wove for him out of plastic yarn when i was in junior high school and that he had still used every day though it was much repaired, a gold ink pen that i had given to him one christmas when he became a lawyer and a jar of pennies that he was saving for cheo two. i believe that my brother and sister got even less. i know that my sister has his guitar but he gave it to her while he was still alive because he had cut the tendons in some of his fingers in an accident and could play no more to his own satisfaction.

my father carried a picture of my mother in his wallet until the day he died, an old, faded and signed snap shot picture of her when she was but seventeen years old, a picture with a flower in her hair, long and thick and glossy black. he was sixty three years young.

five and almost twenty years have passed by now

i do not visit his grave

it took five years

that first and only time

One4DeBrovahs

before i went there
where he rests
warm and secure in the earth
cold and lonely

i found the approximate spot to stop the car
i got out; looking at the map they gave me
at the cemetery's gate
and then i simply knew where he was
i never found him on the map
but he was calling to me
i walked straight there
to his resting place

leroy solder it said on the small stone plaque
date of birth – february 14, 1919
valentines day
date of death - june 13, 1982

bits and tiny pieces of him swirled about me
hello, how are you, how have you been
look at you, oh, how i've missed you son
his longing and lonely cry
filled my ears and heart
deafening me

One4DeBrovahs

his soul was long departed
but i am flesh of his flesh
blood of his blood
even now
like magnets
we are drawn together
after all is said and done

i sat with him for awhile
i shed quiet tears and held him close
we made our gentle peace
said our loving goodbyes
i went away again

i have not been back there
these last twenty years
it is on another coast
and life has taken me away
from there
but i must go back there
someday soon, soon

just today, just today
i sent a prayer into the night sky
telling him that i understood at last
that he did the best he could

One4DeBrovahs

with so much to learn
in so little time
a blink of the eye
in times' eternal march

i hope and pray that my sons
will one day know the same
about their father
when i too
am out of time
in the end
when i too
have run out of time
in the end
at last

HEART

snapshots

it is a very troubling thing, this losing one's light and essential source of comfort so suddenly. somehow, i was not prepared for it really. i knew she was failing and old and suddenly so little and sweet and weak and sick and all of that but her spirit was so strong and her intelligence so sharp that she seemed a force of nature to me, like always. after all, she has been burning brightly for all my life and now she is gone. i cannot seem to think of her as being dead. not really. it is taking me a real effort to get that idea firmly planted in my head. every time i think about her, i get these pictures and visual images, snatches of conversations and bits of laughter or her wisdom or whatever i got from her at that time and then i stop to think that she is gone and it wigs me out a little. i guess it takes time.

in truth, i did not fully realize how central she was to my life and thinking until she was no longer there. not that i did not try to be a good son and stay in touch with her on a pretty much daily basis these last few years. i did that and i am so happy that i did. we would talk about little stuff and big stuff all the time. particularly about ayida, my sister: whenever i complained about some slight she seems to revel in inflicting on me these days, she would always say: "now, you know your sister is a nut" and tell me to ignore her shit and love her the best that i could because she was my only living sibling now. i would always remind her that she was not only my sister but she was most certainly her daughter first and foremost and that would cause a pause while she thought about that and then we would both sigh and laugh it off and go on to more pleasant subjects.

these snapshots keep coming.

my earliest coherent memories center around the time my older brother and sister (the oldest by a little more than a year) went off to school and i stayed home because i was a few years too young. i thought that this was most unfair but the upside was that i got to spend the morning with my mother, all by myself. i would be awake before her and i would drag my blankie and pillow into her room and would curl up on the floor at the foot of her bed and go back to sleep until she woke up a little later. she would always awaken me as she passed from the bedroom and then we would sit in the kitchen together while she woke up in the morning sun.

i made her first cup of coffee every morning. i was so proud and grown up. i would take her order and then i would drag a chair to the stove to stand on and put on a small pot of water to boil. i would watch it like a hawk until the little bubbles appeared. during this time of watching, i would always ask her how she wanted it and she would tell me to put one full spoonful of instant coffee and two sugars in the cup and then add a little cream. i would carefully pour the water over a spoonful of hills brother's instant coffee and add the sugar. i would then (always) ask her how much cream she wanted and she would (always) tell me: "oh, just make it your color, honey" and i would pour the cream carefully with one hand and my other hand held up to the cup until i had a match. it was our morning ritual.

to this day, i drink my coffee with two sugars and a little cream that matches my color.

snapshot

i was sure i was going to be homeless and all alone forever very soon.

see, i was looking for something under her bed and i could not see because it was dark. i was about seven or eight and the logical thing to do was to light a match and hold it under the bed. of course, the mattress caught fire. i did not panic. i went to the kitchen to get a glass of water and calmly walked back to her bedroom to pour it on the growing problem (more smoke than fire at that point, i remember). naturally, this did little to quell the ever expanding blaze. i began to hurry up with the glasses of water and began to finally run back and forth between the sink and the bedroom.

my sister, who was babysitting me that night, noticed me running past the doorway that led to the living room where she was watching television or reading one of her ever present books and asked me what was going on. i stopped long enough to tell her that there was a small fire in mother's room. my sister bolted up and in and after surveying the situation, called the fire department and called out to a neighbor who came and wrestled the burning bed out of the house and into the front yard. he then turned on the hose and put out the flames. a few minutes later, the fire department trucks drove up and all these heavy jacketed, helmeted and boot wearing firemen charged at our front door with axes raised so they could gain entry quickly. luckily, my sister saw them coming and opened the door before any damage was done and told them that the situation was well in hand and pointed out the soggy mattresses sitting in our front yard. after inspecting the house to be sure, the fire department departed.

now, at this point, i should explain that my mother was out for the evening. she had gone to a party. she was never a heavy drinker but when she did get a little "tipsy", as she called it, she was given to being very affectionate. though very gentle and intelligent and very much a good single most of the time type mother (which means she worked long hours at some job to keep us fed and housed, no good husband on premises or not) she did not lavish affection on us for the most part. she was good for a kind word always and a hug when needed but, usually she was pretty reserved. except for when she was "tipsy" and that happened at home only when she gave a party. then she would call out to whichever of us three children was passing closest to her and say: "come hea and give yo' mutha a kiss, baaybey" in an exaggerated southern accent that she did not possess having been born and raised in los angeles and then we would have to endure being very publicly hugged to her bosom and smacked soundly and loudly and messily (especially if she was wearing lipstick and since this embarrassment only happened during one of her parties, of course she was always wearing lipstick) on the cheek. funny, but i never wiped the lipstick off whenever i was the victim. i would wear it the rest of the night until bedtime, always. i remember the smell and the sticky weight of it on my face and smile.

at any rate, she was returning from a party that night and had been dropped off a few houses down from home and as she made her way up the sidewalk to our walkway, she noticed the smoldering remains of a bed on the front lawn but the only thing she thought about it very briefly was that someone in the neighborhood had had a problem. she was pretty tired (and a little "tipsy") and her only goal was to crawl into her bed and get some rest. she tripped into the house and headed for her bedroom only to discover that there was no bed. everything became clear and suddenly she was "tipsy" no longer. she went in to see my sister and my sister told her what had happened.

it was late by now and yet i was still awake. i was just sitting in my room on my bed, still fully dressed. i had already packed my few treasured belongings and a change of clothes and a pair of pajamas in a shopping bag which was sitting next to me on the floor. i knew that i was going to have to leave the house pretty soon and just wanted to be ready. i did not know where i was going to go but i was ready. i had visions of me walking along a lonely road with my bag over my shoulder on a stick like the hoboes in the movies always did.

the door to my room opened and there was my mother. she did not say anything for a minute and then she came and sat down beside me. finally, after taking in my smoke stained face with the paths of shed tears coursing down my cheeks, she said; "it looks like you've had a long night". i answered that this was indeed the case. she thought about that for a second and then said: "maybe we should get some sleep then". and she lay down in my bed, pulling me with her and wrapped her arms around me and we went to sleep. she never did mention that bed. not ever. not until i was a grown man and even then i had to bring it up myself.

snapshot

there is that christmas…

my birthday is in june and my father promised me a 10 speed bicycle. this was in february or march and for the next few months visions of this splendid machine filled my every daydream. i boasted to my friends at school and at home about it modestly because that was how it was done in my neighborhood consisting of families with modest means. you could talk about the things you had or were going to have but you had to be careful not to make the less fortunate feel too badly. most of my friends had bikes but they were either gearless or were of the variety then known as sting rays - perfect for hook sliding or curb jumping and very cool, to be sure, but totally clunky, pedestrian and outclassed when compared to the sleekness and sophistication of a 10 speed, as far as i was concerned.

my birthday came and went and no bicycle appeared. my father told me that he was having hard financial times and would make good on his promise for christmas.

my dad did not live with us. he and my mother had split up when i was a baby but he was there on the periphery most of the time. he would pick us up every other sunday for a movie or an afternoon of exploring some of the other attractions offered in the los angeles area (disneyland, knott's berry farm, pacific ocean park, marine land, mount baldy, allavera street, etc…) and then we would have dinner at his house with him and his new wife, margaret. he was always fun and generous and loving. he taught us crazy songs to pass the time as we drove along. he worked in construction and always drove a new car, unlike the beaters my mother usually had. a promise of a 10 speed bicycle from him meant only the best quality since my father bought only the best of anything. my new bike promised to be the sensation of the neighborhood.

my boasting continued but was now somewhat muted. the visions, however, intensified to a feverish level. i even dreamed about the wind blowing in my face as i sailed down some hill or reached impossibly incredible speeds by manipulating the gears that i truly did not understand and have not even yet mastered, i must admit. my feet were a blur as i peddled, night after night in my dreams, as i flew faster and faster.

the day before christmas, my father breezed through and handed the three of us five dollars each. by way of an explanation he said that christmas was kind of slim this year, meaning of course, that he did not have much in the way of extra money to spend. at this point, he excused himself, saying that he was in a bit of a hurry because he was taking his new wife's niece, sheryl – who had recently come to live with them in their new house out in the suburbs, far away from our little dwelling in the heart of the ghetto - to disneyland and he made good his escape.

now, don't get me wrong. five dollars was a lot of money to me then (and sometimes, even now it ain't too shabby to tell the truth). it represented an endless supply of penny candies and r.c. cola's and pickled pig feet and beef jerky and polly seeds that allowed you the pleasure of spitting the leftover husks all over the place as your tongue became raw from all the extra salt and monster sour pickles, judiciously chosen for juiciness and size, which you could manage to make last for hours of eating enjoyment if you were careful or sweet and sour seeds and dried ginger that i used to buy from the japanese store a few blocks away. no, it was a lot of money. but – it was not a 10 speed bike by any stretch of the imagination.

my 12 year old world had been dramatically altered and reduced with a crash. i could not even think straight. i went to my room and sat in the closet with the door closed, as i was wont to do when i was really upset and needed to be completely alone.

complicated gears, gone. stylish handlebars, like ram's horns, gone. sleek leather seat, just made for my narrow behind, gone. wind in my face as i raced, gone.

i don't know how long i sat in the dark but it was a long time. i must have cried but i don't really remember doing so. at some point, my big brother steve opened the door and asked if i had the five dollars daddy had given me. he explained that he and my sister were going to combine the total amount to buy a special present for mother. i gave the money up without a comment and he went away, closing the door softly behind him, leaving me alone in the blackness.

it was christmas eve and i finally went to bed. i was twelve and my sleep was sound that night. in the morning, before first light, it was christmas after all is said and done and i was twelve years young, i woke up and made my way into the living room to where the christmas tree sat blinking and filling the living room with colored light and the smell of pine needles. i did not expect too much in the way of presents because my mother never had any extra cash for extravagances. usually, we got clothes and one or two special things that came from the list we would dutifully present each year, hoping, always hoping. somehow, she always managed to pick the right one or two special things so christmas was never a bad time at all. she always seemed pleased with the bottle of "exotic" perfume we would buy for her at the local drugstore.

it took me a moment to process what i was looking at.

parked on it's kickstand and sitting in front of the tree was a deep red, sparkling in the blinking multi-colored lights (that we draped over the lopsided tree we always seemed to get and saved from year to year in tattered boxes that were stuffed in a closet the other 11 months of the year) and complicated completely beyond my comprehension, 10 speed bicycle with a ribbon tied around the handle bars, like a ram's horns.

i was afraid to get any closer because it looked so beautiful from where i stood in the doorway. i was not even sure it was for me but i knew it was for me. also, i was afraid to get closer because i did not want to really see it clearly because it was probably used and nicked up and not nearly as beautiful as my imagination was leaping to conclude and also, the moment was so sublime i wanted the illusion to last forever. nobody else was up so i inched closer. a used one would have been ok. i understood how little money we had and was accustomed to these mental and emotional accommodations. all poor children are. we grow up tougher than old shoes but our heart of hearts are just as tender as baby jesus', you know.

as i got closer, the bike looked better and better. it was brand, spanking new. neither a scratch nor a patch of age induced rust on it. i did not touch it. i dared not touch it because it was not officially mine yet. that had to wait until everyone was up and that might not be for hours and hours. but – i looked at every inch closely, up and down. it was a deep metallic red color with little speckles of gold. the gears were all there. the handle bars were there. the taut, finely crafted leather seat was there. the indication of speed and style and elegance was all there.

merry christmas to me. it was mine.

during the night, my mother had made call after call to friends and relatives all over the city. someone knew someone who had hot bikes for sale. the ghetto network which allows us a little breathing room was alive and well, thank you very much. she had pulled together the cash she did not have to make this purchase because she had heard my heart break and would not let it stand that way. she would not have it. she moved heaven and earth for me. my brother and sister gave up their five dollars and so did i, for a very special and precious gift for my mother.

snapshot

not all the pictures are limited to just my mother, though they are all about her in my mind now.

gumbo is like chicken soup in that it is good for what ails you. albondigas soup (meatball soup - mexican style) is another dish like that. when i grew up and i would get the blues, i would always go and have a nice big bowl of gumbo or albondigas soup and i would immediately feel better.

when i was a boy, my family (which is quite large and raucous) would gather and we would have outdoor cookouts. the host family would buy a brand new 50 or 100 gallon metal trash can and build a fire in the backyard. they would build the basic stock and then as everyone arrived each would add their special ingredient to the mix until we had a huge, steaming pot of gumbo. some members were known for sausages or oysters or shrimp or whatever it was that they made or knew where to buy that was better than anyone else and they would bring it with them and when they showed up a cheer would go through the crowd and a list somewhere would be checked off for that ingredient. they would also fry catfish and make hot french bread dripping in butter and garlic and other dishes (many of my family were from louisiana) like bbq and beans and salads too numerous to name and finally the feast would be on. by the end of the day, what with the music (always live) and the drinking and the eating and the talking and the laughing and the small intrigues, the gumbo would be down to the last few gallons and everyone who wanted some would take a little home with them in a plastic container which they would bring from their cars.

by this time, the sun would have long ago set and the southern california night air would carry a slight nip and sweaters would magically appear along with the lights in the backyard (we were free to go indoors but we seldom did) and the children would be sleepy and cranky after a long, hard day playing with the cousins (so many cousins it was hard to count them all but we knew them all) and then the families would go their separate ways home again, full and satisfied until the next time.

half of my family seemed to be either policemen or criminals, in any case, most of the men carried guns and smoked cigars or filterless cigarettes and always they talked and laughed loud with each other (but with the children they were all unfailingly patient, kind and gentle - no matter whose child it was we would all leave there with a few dollars in change jingling in our pockets that they would slip to us for some reason, payment for running an errand, delivering a message to a wife or other small favors) and they would gather about the cooking fire, telling one outrageous lie after another one and to each other and sometimes the - edited for content and company – truth about one another, which was even more outrageous than the lies most times and always very funny in any case and they all drank ice cold pabst's blue ribbon or miller's high-life beer from the can or bottle and, later, as the sun set, they drank johnny walker black or red from short water glasses with about an inch of the brown liquid at the bottom and when they sipped, they all held out their pinky fingers daintily (in most cases they had diamond rings on them, glinting in the light). many of them wore their watches with the faces on the inside of their wrists and since i was at the height of their wrists i was acutely aware of it and as soon as i got a watch of my own, i wore mine that way too. my sons today do the same thing sometimes. i thought they were the strongest, most beautiful men in the world and i wanted so much to be like them when i grew up.

the women were all beautiful too and gracious and matter of fact and very southern the way black women can be no matter where they are born and they would gather together to talk and laugh quietly amongst themselves the way all women everywhere seem to do and they played cards like experts (bid whist - a game i still find beyond comprehension) and every now and again, they would be called upon to settle a dispute among the men or the children or to bandage a bloody knee or arm or finger or to pass out a much needed hug or kiss to either men or children (sometimes the same thing, really) and they would not do the cooking, no - that was left to the men, this outside cooking stuff, though they kept an eye trained and did have very definite opinions about the process and were not shy to express them if necessary.

jean, my mother was the most beautiful of the women, though she wore it well. she was even more beautiful than her twin sister, noreen. she was very strong and smart and stylish and down to earth and never flaunted how most of the men were secretly or openly in love with her. she had that power yet never abused it. all the husbands and boyfriends were safe and all the wives relaxed. they were sisters and brothers and aunts and uncles and cousins and friends for life and there was never any mess.

i always knew where she was because it was important to me to know where she was. she always knew where i was and what i was doing too. all she had to do was to raise an eyebrow in my direction and i would respond immediately in whatever was the appropriate action to be taken at the time to lower that eyebrow. that was how it was at that time to be a child. and - that is how my childhood went, surrounded by this tribe of tall man and lovely women, mostly gone now.

snapshots

every time i think of my mother, who was at the center of it all, those times come back to me in full force and i have to catch my breath for a minute, blink back the tears that are always at the ready but have curiously not fallen often and i must take a look around me to remember that i am still here and life is a continuous thing and it is not over by a long shot and so it is ok to remember those days as long as i remember that too.

i go on into the silent future.

the love i have known is not rare. but it is an important distinction to say that i have been loved and cherished for all of my life and to know who carried the largest share of it. women have come and gone for me. children i have met along the way and their love sustains me now. but - my mother was always there with a love as steady as my heartbeat. no matter where i was, no matter what i was doing, i could rely on that one constant in this ever changing vista that is my life. it has not stopped, this mother's love. yes, i feel it even now enveloping me and still holding me aloft. the word forever comes to mind and takes on new meaning. the physical absence, though, is hard enough to bear. if i had not faith and understanding of the nature of eternity, i don't know if i could do more right now than stare off into space for a while.

the depth of feeling is hard to imagine but so easy to reach each and every day and every late at night before i sleep.

tears on the page, blood from my heart...

snapshots

PART III. SPIRIT

One4DeBrovahs

SPIRIT

two emperors

love doesn't politely ask

it just strikes…

i had just moved into my new place and was getting to know the neighborhood when i saw him just sitting on a bench across the street in the shade filled recess between melnia cass blvd. and windsor street. he was just sitting peacefully and staring into space as i passed him by. i spoke and he looked at me and his warm brown eyes were filled with soulful longing, the same as my cocker spaniel bridgette when i was a boy. he only smiled at me and nodded his head slightly. i fell in love just like that.

over the next few weeks, i saw him occasionally and then i realized that he actually slept on the bench where i first saw him. one day, i took him a plate of food and a few dollars for whatever he might need it for and i knew that it would go for drink because that is what he did all day, as he was able. i tend not to judge too harshly because i have been there and i know that sometimes drink is all we have and we all have our burdens and his seemed very heavy already.

we talked a bit that time, after he had eaten. he spoke softly and intelligently and had a slight accent. he was from ethiopia. so am i, on my mother's side of the family. he told me that he slept on this bench in this between-place because he felt safe in the neighborhood, among his own people, that nobody ever bothered him. he told me his name was haile and it took me away, that name.

when i was a teenager, i made a pilgrimage of sorts. i went to ethiopia. during the time i was there, i met the emperor three times. the first time was as part of a large group and the second time was more personal.

i was in a place called harare shopping for a soft african cloth for my mother when all of the women started making this high pitched sound. it was not unpleasant but i did not know what it meant. everyone stopped whatever they were doing and started to run in the same direction. i did not know what was going on but in my young and american mind, i had visions of lions attacking so i thought it best to go with the flow and so i ran too. after a bit of confusion, i learned that the emperor was coming, the emperor was coming and that sound made by the women was the signal that everyone else knew meant only that one thing.

we all waited by the side of the road and sure enough, after a few seconds an entourage of elegant cars approached slowly and sitting in the back of a rolls royce convertible all by himself was the emperor of ethiopia, the longest reigning monarch in the world, the lion of judah who traced his lineage back to little david who slew goliath, the king of kings to my mind; haile sallassee. he was smiling and waving and tossing money to the crowd. when he came abreast of where i was standing, he glanced at me standing there, obviously out of place with my levis and tennis shoes and t-shirt and my then huge afro and then he quickly said something to his driver and the line of cars came to a sudden halt. he looked at me for a beat or two further and then motioned for me to come forward. i looked around to see who he was motioning to because it couldn't have been me and the people behind me started to laugh gently and then someone softly pushed me forward and kind people around me smilingly pointed at me, telling me to go to him.

i stepped to his car and he smiled at me and spoke to me in amharic. i did not understand him and said that i was sorry, i had forgotten the language. he raised an eyebrow and then asked me in english where i was from and i haltingly told him that i was from los angeles, california, usa and i addressed him as "your highness" and then i started to cry. he looked at me for a few seconds and then he said: "l. a.? nice town." then he handed me an "ethi" dollar, patted my hand and said: "welcome home, son" and then he motioned for his entourage to continue and he rode away.

with those three words, "welcome home, son", he changed my life. the totality of the price of the african slave trade came crashing down on me personally and i suddenly knew the terrible, terrible cost. the long, long four hundred years of death and pain and suffering came to a sharp point in me and then it was soothed away by a gentle smile from a king. i was home again, a stranger no longer, a stranger from myself, a man out of time and step my whole life growing up in los angeles, born in watts and feeling an uncomfortable familiarity with i knew not what but i knew that i was not an anglo-saxon and the sensibilities of that dominant culture did not resonate with me nor with anyone i knew, we were "other" and though offered the chance to throw off our foreignness, we did not, we kept it close to ourselves and kept to ourselves even when offered the chance to blend in and from it sprang our music and art and food and dress and way of looking at the world with an amused detachment and sense of sadness that permeated every waking moment and an understanding that god was always around and involved. with those three words, "welcome home, son" i discovered my african-ness and have never been the same person i was before. my back and shoulders straightened and my heart swelled with the pride of knowing who and what i was. i was a child of the sun, the moon, the stars and the endless plains.

after he had driven away and several people smiled at me and seemed to understand my embarrassing tears, i looked at the money the emperor had handed to me and realized that it had a picture of himself printed on it and for some reason that made me laugh, just to think of it, the man had his own money, and the moment was broken and time began again and the incident became part of the fabric, the weave of my being. i put the bill in my wallet and carried it there for over twenty years.

as i was sitting with this haile, though, the one who sleeps on a bench near where i had just moved in, that is where i went briefly, back to that dusty roadside and that frozen moment in time. we chatted companionably for awhile and then i went back inside to wash the dish that had held his food. his manner reminded me of the quiet dignity of that other haile. he was humble yet very clear and strong in his own way too. he knew who he was and his current condition notwithstanding, he was sure of himself and at peace with the world.

i carried that bill with the portrait of the lion of judah for over twenty years. i carried it in my wallet until i met a beautiful little boy in columbia, maryland who was dying and then i gave it to him for strength.

though i no longer live right across the street from where haile sleeps, i see him from time to time and if i have anything to give, i always give it. he has never asked me for anything at all. one day, though, i did not have any money when i saw him. i apologized for not giving him anything that time and he smiled and told me that my love was enough, more than enough and he hugged me and told me that he loved me too. riches come in many forms and on that day i was a trillionaire.

love doesn't politely ask

it just strikes…

SPIRIT

saint alice

for the good you did right here…

a friend sent me a notice of her passing over via email. since i don't read the newspapers or watch television or even listen to the radio, sometimes the grapevine is my only source of news unless it is prominently featured on yahoo. i do take a look at the news on the internet most days but sometimes i might miss three or four days in a row because i don't go online for one reason or another.

this story touched me on many levels. i loved alice coltrane. i loved her music, with all its intricate nuance and majestic sweep. you always knew that she had an orchestra, a celestial orchestra going in her head when she played. to listen to her musical genius was to know the divine nature of things and to know that god was alive and well and always around. she was plugged into the natural current that connects us all and her music was about that and about prayer.

as a young man, she ruined me as a musician.

all i ever wanted to do was to play a little music. well…, that is not quite right. i wanted to play a lot of music. i dreamt of playing the organ, like jimmy smith on "who's afraid of virginia wolf" at first and i used to pretend that i was playing instead of him when i listened to it over and over again when no one was around. it caused me to dream even then, music did. then one day i was looking through my older brother's albums and i saw a silhouette of a man sort of slumped over and playing a trumpet and i asked him who this was and he said simply: "that's miles". i fell in love right then and there with him and have been very faithful lo these many years. i remember that in the liner notes, the writer was trying to express the quality that miles possessed, of his understated power and patience and he used a spanish expression that translated badly to describe a man walking gently on eggshells without damaging them; in essence that he had to have tremendous strength and control to be that soft yet passionate at the same time. in listening to his muted trumpet as he played poetry in sound, i understood exactly what the writer meant.

as i grew up other players caught my eye and i sort of divided my love to cover them as well but especially to completely embrace john coltrane and his hot, hot torrents of arpeggios and scales, sheets of sound one critic called it and once again, the description fit. somewhere in there, i heard alice for the first time on harp and the addition of that sound just blew me away because that must be what heaven sounds like, yes? sweeping, swirling, sweet note after note plucked fast in an echoed waterfall and slow and pure like a soft stringed guitar, only fuller; much, much fuller. her albums were vistas unknown or only dreamt of on special nights, a spiritual remembrance, perhaps. i used to sit in the dark and listen to her albums all the time and transcend effortlessly.

when i was nineteen, i made a trip to ethiopia. i was learning to become a teacher of meditation and yoga and the course lasted almost four months. besides the classes and lectures, we did seemingly endless rounds of meditation and yoga for many, many hours through the day and into the nights. it was a very special time.

i had my flute with me and i took brief breaks and spent a little time looking out of my window and played quietly what i was feeling and seeing and becoming. one day, a buzz started because alice coltrane was coming to the place where the course was being held. i must have been excited but i don't remember thinking much about it because i am from los angeles and famous people are always around; they have to live somewhere and drive somewhere and shop somewhere and eat somewhere and you can't help but see them from time to time so we tend to be a little blasé about things like that, i guess.

she came and went into seclusion immediately. she was very religious and apparently she was on a self imposed retreat of some kind. the days went by and i continued my routine of meditation, yoga and playing to the africa that i could see. one night, she came among us and we all shyly met her or greeted her and then she surprised me by walking up to me and asking me if i was the flautist. i admitted that i was indeed the culprit and stared to apologize for disturbing her meditations and she said that at first she thought it was angels, celestial beings making such beautiful music and then she found out it was me. this was a long time ago, over thirty five years now and i know i must have said something but i cannot bring to mind what it was, though i can still recall how it felt, the sheer elation and humility all at once crowding around my heart and then she further astounded me by asking me if i wanted to play a concert with her the next night. needless to say, i agreed that i thought that playing a concert with her was indeed a fine idea.

the next day, i spent most of the day with alice. we walked the countryside together for hours and she talked of little inconsequential things most of the time. she noticed every person, every flower and tree and bird and blade of grass and insect and animal, it seemed, and was enamored of it all. she would point out something and then would talk about some holy aspect of it. i remember being surprised that she sort of mumbled when she talked and that she laughed a lot. every now and again, she would talk a little about the music we would play that night and would sing me a melody to remember. just a short phrase or snatch of tune and i would sing it back to her a few times and then we would sing it together. i did not have my flute with me and she certainly was not carrying her piano, organ or harp. we merely had our voices and our hearts joining in song along an ethiopian dirt road.

that night we played. from somewhere a drummer appeared and someone on bass. i have no recollection of them at all, i must admit. i was hyper aware of everything else though and very calm and still inside and the air seemed thick and slow. we began to play one of the melodies she had sung to me and we were off and flying. we played several of her tunes in succession and i was surprised that i remembered them all with just a few notes of introduction. we played so hard and fast that i was dizzy. i looked back at her at one point and she was hunched over her keyboards and comping chords like a mad woman. she looked up at me in deadly earnest, urging me on, telling me silently to play my song with hers. i felt that i was riding the crest on a huge wave. i was on a metaphysical surf board and if i missed just one step, one note, i would be swallowed alive and it was exhilarating because i did not miss one step or one note and then she began the chords to a love supreme. i did not have time to think about it, i just played it and played it and played it until i could play no more and then the music was over.

the people in the audience cheered and clapped but i was too spent, too dizzy and too spaced out to really respond. my mind was still racing and the music was still flowing inside my head and through my veins, pulsing throughout my whole body. we made our way off stage and then she turned to me and fixed me with her very intense and so kind eyes for a few seconds with a small smile playing about her lips and then she pressed the fingers of her right hand to my chest, hard, touching my heart and said: "keep playing". that was all she said and then she nodded her head once and smiled at me again and was gone into the crowd. people slapped me on the back and seemed quite amazed and pleased with my playing and with the music.

i don't remember the sequence of events of the next few days but soon she was gone away. i did not see her again, that i remember. i went back to playing to the african days and nights and air. eventually, the course was over and i made my way back to america from so far away and so much at home. it was a strange returning because i had lost the knot in my shoulders that had always been with me and i had seen my people in their own country and i had discovered that our gentleness, laughter and shyness were a shared trait, even after all that had passed in horror in our new land. the ride home on the san diego freeway was surreal because i was relaxed and traveling through a different space and time, from all the meditation and yoga and also i had discovered my african-ness somewhere along the way.

another thing changed for me. i could not play in clubs anymore. i still went to them to hear others play but i could not do it myself. it seemed profane to me now, with all the smoke and drink and talking and rough edged life lived so fast. music was inextricably tied to quiet and personal prayer now and i realized that it always had been so for me. most of the time a musician plays alone anyway. somewhere in a room we all practice the scales and chords and patterns and notes that we hear or read and who is it who is there to listen besides ourselves, if not god? it is a joyful noise we make. in fact, late at night, i used to play with a mockingbird that lived in a tree beside my bedroom window. he taught me many sly tricks and i taught him a few as well.

i did see alice one other time. though i heard of her often enough i did not go to see her nor seek to play with her again. she had established an ashram somewhere in southern california. i didn't go because i was shy, i guess. the one other time i did see her was outside of the rose bowl in pasadena. as i was making my way into the stadium to listen to the music that would be played there that day, i saw her sitting quietly on a bench all alone up against the stadium wall, bathed in the warmth of the sun. i was with friends and i excused myself and went to her. we looked at each other for a second or two and she smiled. i knelt on one knee and i took her hand and held it to the side of my face and then i kissed it gently, reverently and called her "divine mother" and then i went away. she actually did not say anything at all; she just smiled at me with tenderness and reticent surprise. i re-joined my friends who asked me who she was and who were looking at me strangely because i was not the type of young man who knelt in the dirt for anyone. i don't think i even answered them because my mind and my heart were filled with swirling strings and compelling rhythms.

life took me away, finally. i tried to make the music of my dreams several times but something, usually me, got in the way and before i knew it, twenty years passed in quietness before i awoke with a determination to make it happen and to hear it, the music, played at last.

i bought musical instruments on layaway and then i began to practice and to make a joyful noise yet again, though this time there was no mockingbird to guide me. the patterns and scales and chords were all i had. a teacher appeared and then another, giving me instruction and tisk, tisk tisking my terrible form and habits. somewhere along the way, the words started to flow and i found my voice again and then the tabernacle of the theatre where i could play my songs was revealed to me. riotous angels joined me and here we are, ready to get busy.

alice coltrane may have ruined me as a musician, this may be true, but she also taught me as a simple child of god to make a joyful noise for my creator that will echo forever and ever and ever and ever…, just like her.

selah…

SPIRIT

my god, by god

i sang a solo in the church choir when i was but a tike, no older than four or five. "he's got the whole world in his hands". complete with gestures that i practiced alone in my room in front of a big mirror until i had it right, in preparation for my big moment. i made a big circle for "the whole world". i held my two hands together as if cupping something for "in his hands". i pointed out people in the audience for "he's got you and me brother, he's got you and me sister, in his hands". i was cute. i knew it because everyone was looking at me with tilted heads and indulgent smiles while i sang in my high childish voice, totally unafraid because i was among people i had grown up seeing every sunday and sometimes in between. besides; my mother was there and so was my older brother and sister. i wasn't nervous in the least. i was proud to be singled out.

that's probably my earliest memory of pondering god; the sunday school lessons about our lord and savior, jesus christ, only partially absorbed in truth, because i was very young. but it was there that i first learned of the father and the son and the holy ghost (which always scared me a little even if i didn't understand it because though holy it was still a ghost and the only friendly ghost i knew was casper who was just a little boy trying to make friends among the living and who made me feel sad for some reason in spite of being sweet and harmless and, yes, friendly). i remember liking the smells and the music and dressing up. i don't remember the preaching at all but i remember the rustle of clothes and the sounds of so many feet on the hardwood floors. i definitely remember the food that sometimes came after. nobody lays a spread like church going sisters.

not long after that, when i was about five or six years old, my mother gathered the three of us in the living room of our little house in watts and told us that she was not going to do to us what had been done to her and her sister. she said that they had been going to church every sunday since she and her twin, norene, were little girls and that she was sick of it and was not going anymore. it was her opinion that these so-called christians had three faces: one they showed in church, another they showed at home and the third, their real face, they showed in the streets. she was tired of the hypocrisy and wasn't going to participate in it any longer.

she remarked that we all knew where the church was located and were free to go if we choose to or we were free not to go if we chose not to, that it was entirely up to us. the church was about two or three blocks from our house and that was a safe enough distance for a small child to go alone, let alone with his big sister and big brother, because we lived in a neighborhood where everybody knew who you were and where you lived and, for sure, knew who your people were (especially your mother, it seemed) and would sometimes go so far as to correct your behavior away from home by reminding you of those facts. it really does take a village…

i don't even remember if we (my brother, sister and me) had a discussion about it but we never went back to church again, none of us. just like that. i did not grow up in the normal african american tradition of attending church on sunday or even grow up thinking about myself as a christian because my mother gave me a choice. although, sometimes when under peer group pressure, i would occasionally identify myself as such, the truth was that i was not and am not to this day a christian. i have never been baptized. i am nothing at all, really, in terms of religion.

the strangest part of it was that it did not mean that we were raised to not believe in god. that there was a god, there was little doubt but there no discussion given to the subject overall. it was just understood. my mother was not the type to call on "jaysus" in trying times or to praise the "lawd" when happy. she called on her inner strength in times of trouble and praised and kissed and hugged us when she was happy. religion and things related to it; talk of god, the devil and all of that ceased when my mother turned away from religion. when i asked her about it one day, she went so far as to offhandedly assure me that angels did in fact exist and that they lived among us and she even provided me a way of proving it for myself. and - i have done so a few times over the years. so, i can tell you with all sincerity that there is a god and that angels do indeed exist and live among us. this i know from personal experience and not because the bible tells me so.

perhaps it is this lack of formal guidance on the matter which has led me to view the world as i do; full of wonder and joy most days. i recognize the miracle of life with every step i make and marvel at the wisdom and symmetry about me with every breath i take. every beat of my heart is accompanied by a celebration of the divine and my hellos are filled with humility and grace and love. i can see that we are all connected to each other and that we are all also connected to that which is above and beyond. god is real and loves us all. this i know with a surety that no words or works of man can ever shake or alter. i have seen it for myself.

maybe i should pause a moment and back up just a little. how did i get to this, you might in all fairness ask? after all, i had no one to teach me the prayers or the hymns to sing in praise. i passed with religious ignorance through my childhood all the way to manhood in the same state. i do not call upon jesus as my personal savior, though i love him dearly just as i love all holy men and women and prophets and the wise and magical ones from all lands and all times. i believe the stories and cherish the knowing.

you see, i have read the bible. i have also read the koran. i have read the upanishads. i have read the teachings of buddha. i have read about confucius. i have savored the yogi's trance. i have read the texts that have been written by those who have seen or even touched the face of god in whichever form they were privileged to see it. the stories never stop and keep being revealed in every generation and in every land. miracles happen every single day.

there was a story not long ago about a young girl who was kidnapped from her ethiopian village. she was taken into the jungle and was being beaten by a group of men who were trying to force her into an unwanted marriage. all of a sudden, two lions emerged from the bush and chased the men away, leaving the girl bloody, injured and alone. the lions sat with her through that day and night and did not leave her side. they kept her safe. when her own people finally found her early the next day and carefully approached, the lions just faded back into the tall trees and grass. they had never touched her, they just sat guard. whenever a new bible is written, this is one of the stories that should be told. it happened just a few months ago, not two or three thousand years ago.

perhaps because i have not grown tired and bored with the repetition of a religious dogma and am not merely going through the motions by now, long since stopping to think what is being said? perhaps because i have been spared the mental pushing and pulling of having to decide who is holier or more righteous because i have not been there to hear it declared? perhaps because i have not had knowledge of my creator handed to me and explained to me by those more in the know, that i have had to think for myself? perhaps i have had to seek understanding through close observation? maybe that's it.

beyond the words raised from the pulpit or printed on pages, though, there is life, the greatest teacher of all. as we travel our long roads, there are signs of the miraculous and holy everyday, like the little girl and the lions. or just thinking about our perfect bodies that can burn almost any fuel and keep working just fine or that we are hurtling through space at hundreds of miles an hour with barely a hair out of place means something, doesn't it? who set this up? in whose image are we made?

who made the orange taste so sweet? who directed the humble bumble bee to its honey making enterprise? who made the fish in the sea? who made the animals roaming the plains? who made the birds that sing me awake each day? who made the sun so regular and warm? who gave us the gift of choice and thought? who gave me music in my soul with which to praise and pray?

there is but one answer. it is not evolution except as the plan began ages ago with magic and was sent on its slow way with love and finely wrought wisdom. something this beautiful is not the result of random chance, this much perfection is not an accident. i may not know the words to the songs that everyone seems to know whenever i have visited a church service as i do every now and again but i know that much. it is not an accident, this world, this life and it has meaning and purpose.

i love churches by the way. i have visited them all over the world, these churches and temples and mosques and holy places. i have been to the first christian church in ethiopia, carved out of solid and living rock. all of the angels and cherubs and even the holy virgin mother and child are painted black there as they are still in many of the orthodox christian churches in russia and other slavic countries and as they were in the churches of europe prior to the time of michelangelo. did you know that? it's true.

there is a church in germany, le dome, that took six hundred years to build and then the builders ran out of money and rested for one hundred years. finally they raised the funds for completion and it took another hundred years to finish the spires. it was the largest building in the entire city of cologne by far and it was not a small city, even then. during world war two the city was bombed flat, every building destroyed and, yet, that church was left standing and untouched. it was the only structure left in the whole city. you should see it. and – that story should be told too, whenever the new holy tombs are penned.

i love the fact that a people, any people, will build a house of worship within which to come together to praise or to ponder their creator. i have spent many peace filled moments in them, doing just that. but the reason i have not taken up with a religion, despite an abiding love of things spiritual is that i don't wish to be limited. you see, i love churches because of what they are saying about us but i don't believe for one minute that they are houses where god resides anymore than in any other house. why would the creator of the universe and all things beyond it choose to take up residence in something as temporary as a building, no matter how magnificent? it will tumble into dust eventually.

no, i say that god is everywhere, residing in every tree and blade of grass and mountain of stone and ocean deep and white of cloud and blue of sky and in the infinite stars. god is on the breeze blowing across your face as you walk. god is in the cry of a newborn babe and in the stare of the dying and the maimed by war, domestic and foreign. god is in you and in me too. in all of us, our creator resides. in every creature, big and small, god has a residence. we are all churches; all of us are holy places traversing sacred highways.

the god i have come to know and trust and cherish is the property of no one religion or sect or group, no matter how hard they pray or loud they make the claim. in trying to own god, to declare that limited and puny you alone have god's ear and heart, in trying to cut god down to size to fit into your small ornate container, your particular brand, you box yourself off from the true magnificence of god. you cut yourself off from god and you have cut off god from yourself. the wonder is lost to you because you have ceased to wonder.

try this: for everything and everyone you see today say to yourself: "there goes god". just keep saying it. "there goes god". keep saying it until it occurs to you that it is true. it should make you laugh. and then ask yourself what it means. if this is true, how should you behave? how do you honor that inconceivably magical fact? how do you greet one another? how do you treat one another? how can you honor all things, big and small?

it does not mean that you should not go to church this sunday or this tuesday or thursday night either. your coming together brings god into the house. it also means that when you sing the songs, you should sing for the rafters and beyond. when you pray the prayers on bended knee, you should pray for us all. your religion is your style of worship, nothing more nor less than that. style is individual and has always been important. it is not a light thing. it identifies us. i know that.

for me, the style i prefer is the wind in my hair and the sun on my face or the rain falling, wetting my shoulders. i prefer the constant quiet worship of living each day and seeing god's hand in motion everywhere, smelling god in the flowers that grow and seeing his face in you. i may not be a christian, a muslim nor any other nameable thing but i know this much is true and i share it with you in love. jesus wasn't a christian either; you do know that, yes? he was a jew and he was a man, a child of god like you, the son of god, some say and i believe it. i told you that i believe all the stories and cherish the knowing.

and - know this too: that you are always in my prayers as i walk; you and you and you too and all of us together, always in my prayers, always included, just like i practiced it, in the mirror.

amen

One4DeBrovahs

One4DeBrovahs

About the Author

Poet, writer, playwright, screenwriter, performance artist (poetry and music), musician and producer. Cheo Jeffery Allen Solder is originally from Los Angeles, California and currently resides in Geneva, Switzerland and Doha, Qatar. His CD: "Mind, Heart, Spirit: HiStory" has been released on Synchrovision Records and a theatre production of One4DeBrovahs will be produced in 2014 in the US. He recently produced and performed with Desert Bridges, a cultural Non-Profit Organisation and Musical Ensemble in Doha, Qatar with music, compositions and spoken word. Some of his poetry is featured in another Trilingual Press Publication: Liberation Poetry, an Anthology, published September 2011.

Mr. Solder can be reached at: cjas870@yahoo.com